MW00380386

A Seer's Journey

Beyond the Veil

A life lived between Heaven and Earth

Jurena Cook

Heart of David Publishing

Beyond the Veil
Copyright © 2016 by Jurena Cook

Heart of David Publishing
PO Box 294, Grandview, TX 76050

All rights reserved. Brief quotations from this manuscript used in presentations, articles, and books are permitted. However, no part of this publication may be reproduced, stored in a retrieval system, or transmitted in any form or by any means—electronic, mechanical, photocopy, recording, scanning, or any other—without prior permission of Heart of David Publishing or Jurena Cook.

Unless otherwise noted, Scripture verses and passages are from *The Holy Bible, King JamesVersion (KJV).*

Scripture quotations marked:
KJV are taken from King James Version, Copyright 1611
NKJ are taken from New King James Copyright 1982
NLT are taken from New Living Translation, Copyright 1996
NASB are taken from New American Standard Bible, Copyright 1971
NIV are taken from New International Version, Copyright 1978
AMP are taken from Amplified Bible, Copyright 1965 (rev. 1987)
ASV are taken from American Standard Version, Copyright 1901
MSG are taken from The Message, Copyright 1993

Unless otherwise noted, all maps, illustrations, and photos are provided from both personal files and public domain sources.

ISBN #978-0692419922

Editor: Sandy Bloomfield
Cover Design: Joseph Anderson, Michael Severson, Curt Hammell
Interior Artwork: Jurena Cook

Printed in the USA

That the God of our Lord Jesus Christ, the Father of glory,

may give to you a spirit of wisdom and of revelation in the knowledge of Him. I

pray that the eyes of your heart may be enlightened, so that you will know what

is the hope of His calling, what are the riches of the glory of His inheritance in

the saints, and what is the surpassing greatness of His power toward us who

believe. These are in accordance with the working of the strength of His might

which He brought about in Christ, when He raised Him from the dead and seated

Him at His right hand in the heavenly places, far above all rule and authority

and power and dominion, and every name that is named, not only

in this age but also in the one to come.

(Ephesians 1:17-21 NASB)

I have known Pastors Seymour and Jurena Cook for over 25 years. They have proved themselves, over and over again, to be authentic prophetic ministers of the Kingdom of God. I have walked with them through many difficult trials in their journey of faith. Through all of them, they have consistently proved their Godly character, integrity and humble obedience to the call of God upon their lives. Jurena is the singularly most anointed prophetic worship leader that my wife Janet, who trains worship leaders, and I have ever met. She has led worship at our "Panim el Panim" (Hebrew for "Face to Face") prophetic worship gatherings for many years, and has unfailingly brought the gathering to consistently higher and higher levels of worship.

Since a little girl, singing for a nationally known evangelist, Jurena has faithfully stewarded her worship gift, and the evidence of her maturity and fruitfulness, not only as a worship leader but as a minister, is seen in the lives she has touched in America and various nations around the world.

During the course of her walk with the Lord, Jurena has had many angelic encounters and heavenly visitations. These supernatural encounters have always encouraged us and profoundly affected many people. We have come to deeply love and respect both Jurena and Seymour not only as faithful and fruitful servants of the King, but as beloved and dear friends.

I pray that what she shares with you in this book will challenge, encourage and bless you, as you also endeavor to faithfully fulfill the call of God upon your own life.

Dr. Howard and Janet Morgan
Howard Morgan Ministries
Kingdom Ministries International

Heaven has a language that is Spirit to spirit communication. It is difficult for any earthly language to communicate anything Heaven reveals without a hunger and a discerning that is prophetic in its nature. There are no big "I"s or little "you"s in the Kingdom. Jesus said His testimony was the Spirit of Prophecy (Rev 19:10). Prophecy is spirit language. This book is written with no fluff. It is simple! But it is Heaven's simple! The wise in their own eyes will not fathom it. Jesus said it this way, "The hungry shall be filled!" Without that hunger, there is no feeding. May the testimony of JESUS fill and feed you. Because this book took pure faith to write, it imparts true faith simply by its reading. It is rare that a book can impart like the laying on of hands, but this one can, because it carries the testimony of Jesus in its prophecy of Spirit to spirit. May the LORD HIMself invite you deeper to HIS place with you, in the SPIRIT! In truth, what the Lord is sending is His continuous sign and wonder around Jurena and me, and the half has not been told. The visions Jurena is having from the Lord are signs and wonders. It is the language of Heaven – it is how God speaks to Heaven and Earth.

A great sign appeared in Heaven: a woman, clothed with the sun, and the moon under her feet, and on her head a crown of twelve stars…(Rev 12:1 NASB)

The LORD speaks with His signs, and we are still wondering after the LORD Who sent them. This book is filled with signs and wonders.

~ Seymour Cook

Dedication

To Jesus the King, Who gave these words to me, and my mother, who is with Him, and among the great cloud of witnesses cheering for us all to walk in what they now know and understand about the Kingdom of God— and what awaits those who walk with the King of Glory!

Foreword

Jurena Cook first gave me her vision for this book two years ago. She had been referred by an esteemed friend back in Philadelphia, and I was intrigued by the subject matter, so I gave an enthusiastic "yes"—and promptly proceeded to watch my entire world unravel around me.

Now, I am not a shrinking violet, but the spiritual warfare that began to pummel me shortly after we embarked on the adventure that was to become *A Seer's Journey Beyond the Veil* took on a life of its own. Random computer meltdowns, mysterious program malfunctions that cost me the manuscript several times over, and attacks on my health and relationships left me exhausted and wondering if I had heard God on this one. My personal life had its own warfare surrounding a property I bought last year (which I have yet to move onto—did I mention there was warfare?) and trips north as my father's health was failing. I couldn't tell where the hits were coming from. I just wanted them to stop.

My purpose in all this is not to list the many obstacles to seeing Jurena's vision come to pass for sympathy's sake. I just wanted to make two observations.

First, a book that invokes such fury on the enemy's part HAS to carry a pretty powerful anointing. And I believe it does.

Second, as an editor and ghostwriter, I have been privileged to work with everyone from Dr. Phil to ministers working Kingdom harvest fields. Yet never, in my collaborations, have I met a woman whose character is as beautiful as her gifts and anointing. Jurena graciously walked through the minefields with me, never losing patience, never losing her gentle touch. Her maturity of spirit reflects the heart of the God she serves, and I can tell you that she lives out *everything* she teaches. Get ready to go beyond, to soar to new heights in Him.

-Sandy Bloomfield, Editor

Acknowledgments

I would like to acknowledge all those who have stood by me and prayed for me as I worked on this book. They have been with me throughout this process and patiently stayed before the Lord on my behalf. I would like to thank:

Betty Davis, one of the intercessors of our church. She is a mighty, humble woman of God who has been with Seymour and me for 21 years. She faithfully kept me in prayer and comforted me many times with her insights from the Lord. She remembered words I had forgotten and was a ready report to remind me.

Lillian and Gerald McPearson, who have held our arms up for this project, praying tirelessly. Lillian assisted in its development and editing, spending hours transcribing words, then sending me a verbal report so that they would not be forgotten. She and her husband have been faithful and honoring of us in all things.

Michael and Debbie McPearson, who have served and helped us in any way that was needed so that I would be free to write the words the Lord was sending me. She kept up with things through recording and editing, patiently poring through hours of recordings to produce CDs for others to hear.

Bonnie Henderson, who came over to my home three days a week faithfully for years, willing to do whatever was needed to be a blessing to Seymour and me as we have moved forward in this project.

Anita Barnwell, who stood on her feet for hours, recording what happened at Anson Street and at church, capturing the essence of what God was doing. She did everything with a spirit of excellence and an anointing from the Lord.

My entire church family at Messiah's Church—all its members who prayed and gave of themselves so that this book could be published. Their faithfulness and unity of heart will always be remembered by Seymour and me.

Sandy Bloomfield, my editor, who tirelessly worked my book. Through all the challenges and obstacles that were thrown at her, she never gave up. She was a warrior of the Lord on my behalf, and made the publication of this book possible.

Our family for all the love and support that they have given to me in this project. They have encouraged me and have seen only good in me. They have blessed my heart to see Jesus formed in them and their walk with God.

Finally, I would like to thank my wonderful husband Seymour. He is a wind beneath my wings. He believed in me when I did not believe in myself. He had presented me before the Lord as a gift of God. I have always said you can tell a lot about a man by looking at his wife. I am who I am because of him. He has always seen the best in me and encouraged me to let it all come out for the world to see. He is my great love.

Table of Contents

Introduction

We know the veil between God and man has been torn (Mark 15:38).

But how many of us are willing to go beyond our *personal* veils of unbelief, religion, worry, fear, love of money and power, woundedness, unforgiveness, etc.? We have so many veils that blind us from the true and living God—the reality of who He is and how He wants to reveal Himself to us. The work of the cross is complete, but few of us step into the power that is in our salvation. This is true especially for those of us who insist on living in legalism and law. The Word of God is alive—it is able to wash us, nourish us, even to separate our soul from our spirit—but we have missed the point of the work of the cross to release us into the fullness of the life it offers. Instead, we have made the New Testament a book of law instead of the living Word that it is. *He has made us competent as ministers of a new covenant—not the letter but the Spirit; for the letter kills, but the Spirit gives life (2 Cor 3:6 NIV).* Jesus has bought for us the power to overcome and go beyond our personal veils in order to see Him *as He really is,* not *our* image of God for *our* comfort. His Kingdom is not like the kingdoms of this earth. His Kingdom is mighty and full of wonder, power, and glory.

I encourage you before you even start this book to pray and to ask the Lord to help you identify and take away the veils of flesh and every obstacle to seeing in the spirit realm. Ask Him to show you how to rip the veils down in your own temple, even as the ancient temple veil was torn from top to bottom once Jesus fulfilled all requirements and gave us access to the Father and the heavenly throne room itself. Unless we choose to go beyond our veils, we won't understand the way He wants us to go. The Holy Spirit will help you go beyond your personal veils and enter into the secret place that God has prepared for all of His children. We are a living priesthood of believers, but how can we receive our orders unless we enter in to where God is? Otherwise, we remain outside where there is blessing, but there is no intimacy. *Through his death, Jesus opened a new and life-giving way through the curtain into the Most Holy Place (Heb 10:20 NLT).*

We, through Adam, ate from the Tree of the Knowledge of Good and Evil. If we have been redeemed and are being sanctified, our minds love the knowledge of what is good. If the heart is filled with sin, we will love what is evil. A lot of Christian teaching is from the Tree of the Knowledge of Good. We need to speak from the Tree of Life, which is Jesus.

The only way Heaven can come through us is for us to see into Heaven. Otherwise, that which is coming through us is earthly (or we try to live off other people's revelations instead of getting fresh manna ourselves). Jesus taught us to pray, "...thy kingdom come. Thy will be done, as in Heaven, so in earth" (Luke 11:2 KJV). When we see into Heaven and take hold of what is there for us, Heaven is established in earth (in us). Sadly, we have been content to live with our traditional, mental interpretation of Heaven which is simply religion. The Lord cannot be served through religious, mental performance. We must serve the Lord Spirit to spirit. We go from faith to faith, and glory to glory. Each heavenly key leads to new keys. If we can get Heaven's key of prayer, for example, it will give us the next key, which is praise. Praise will give us the next key which is holiness (walking in forgiveness and overcoming self). We must give God's people heavenly keys instead of dead, religious activity. I believe that we should all see in the spirit. We should not be blind.

> *But he, being full of the Holy Spirit looked up steadfastly into Heaven, and saw the glory of God, and Jesus standing on the right hand of God, and said, Behold, I see Heavens opened and the Son of Man standing on the right hand of God. But they cried out with a loud voice and stopped their ears, and rushed upon him with one accord (Acts 7:55-57 ASV);*

After Stephen spoke what he saw, many who did not believe rushed upon him to kill him. They were enraged by the religious spirits that ruled them, and they couldn't bear for the truth to be revealed. The enemy does not want us to see into

Heaven. When you begin to see in the spirit, persecution may arise. I do not think we should seek after visions; but if a vision should come, we should not deny it or disbelieve it. For the most part, the Body of Christ is taught to be afraid of everything spiritual. The Word of God says in John 4:24, *God is spirit: and they that worship Him* ***must worship in spirit and truth*** *(ASV)*.

If you begin to see in the spirit, you can be sure you will have the enemy try to block and tackle every word you say or seek to receive. He will try to derail you with doubt. I have gone through this; it is not easy. You must love truth enough to stand even when it brings division, since you will have those who believe, and others who will think you are deceived, and will leave you. We serve a living God, not a dead idol or an image that we can manage for our purposes or create for our comfort.

> *And the angel of Jehovah appeared unto him in a flame of fire out of the midst of a bush: and he looked, and, behold, the bush burned with fire, and the bush was not consumed (Exo 3:2 ASV).*

Will the Lord not appear to His people today? God said to Moses, "I AM." I want to receive the Father just as He is, don't you? We can be so afraid of being deceived that we don't realize that we are actually living deceived lives by not walking in the totality of the Word. Even though we read, quote, and teach Scripture, too often we skip some of its very foundational pillars, such as: "love your neighbor as you love yourself," "think of what is lovely and of good report," and "forgive and you shall be forgiven." Just as God gave visions to people in the Old and New Testaments, He still gives visions today. He hasn't changed. He's simply waiting on us to prepare ourselves to receive.

How can you tell the difference between false visions and God's visions? One way is that false visions *demand* worship, while true visions *invite* worship.

As I discern visions, I pay attention to the vessel, because visions from the Lord have an impartation. If one is humble and resting in the Lord, they have a sound that can be heard as such. If they are boastful and arrogant, that can be heard, as well. Often, it is just a matter of maturing and allowing some spiritual brokenness to release the sound of Heaven.

True visions always bring change in the heart of the seer. We see this many times in Scripture. It all started with the enemy questioning what the Lord told Adam and Eve about not eating from the tree of the knowledge of good and evil. We know that this was a half-truth. The enemy was wanting to steal their inheritance, which was a face to face walk with God. Jesus came and died to restore what was lost, the walk that Adam and Eve had from the beginning.

Indeed, ownership was stolen. Mankind no longer had God the Father as the only One that they instinctively chose to worship, but rather, satan became the father of sin, and ruler over mankind's fleshly nature. Jesus addressed it this way: *You are wanting to do what your father the devil wants,* (John 8:44) *You are of your father the devil, and you want to do the desires of your father. He was a murderer from the beginning, and does not stand in the truth because there is no truth in him. Whenever he speaks a lie, he speaks from his own nature, for he is a liar and the father of lies. I come to do the work of my father.* The enemy stole their intimacy with God and their access to worship Him.

Jesus was led by the Spirit to regain what was lost (through Adam and Eve), which was the ability to be tempted and yet not be deceived or accepting the enemy's gestures of demanded worship. So the second Adam, Jesus, comes along and the enemy seeks to steal Jesus' inheritance by tempting Him to receive his suggestions, then gifts.

> *Then was Jesus led up of the Spirit into the wilderness to be tempted of the devil...And when the tempter came to him, he said, If thou be the Son of God, command that these stones be made bread. But he answered and said, It is written, Man shall not live by bread alone, but by every word that proceedeth out of the mouth of God (Matt 4:1, 4:3-4).*

The first place the enemy starts the temptation is where he left off with Eve, seeking to lure Jesus to go off of His commitment to fast, separating himself from the spirit, for filling of the body's natural needs: food. The deception here was for Jesus to use His authority without hearing the Father tell Him what to do; to step into the natural first, and in the process, to step out from under His Father's leading. Satan was trying to get him to step into presumption instead of what was written. Jesus spoke and lived these words: *"I only do what I hear the Father tell me to do."*

This is a major key to anyone walking with the Lord. We cannot presume upon the Word for our life's situations. We must always stay connected to the Lord in order to know how to carry out His Word. Otherwise, the enemy will deceive us with the very Word that is written. Psalms 104:27 says, *All creatures look to you to give them their food at the proper time.* The Lord wants us to look to Him, and understand what was written so that when He speaks, we know how to apply that word through relationship with Him. The original design by God was all about hearing and obeying Him. The enemy seeks to get us away from hearing the Father, knowing that if we do not hear Him, then it is easier to deceive us into doing good works, but not doing the will of God.

> *Then the devil taketh him up into the holy city, and setteth him on a pinnacle of the temple, And saith unto him, If thou be the Son of God, cast thyself down: for it is written, He shall give his angels charge concerning thee: and in their hands they shall bear thee up, lest at any time thou dash thy foot against a stone. Jesus said unto him, It is written again, Thou shalt not tempt the Lord thy God (Matt 4:5-7).*

In the second temptation, Jesus replies, *"Thou shall not tempt the Lord thy God."* The enemy was tempting Jesus to have *God* work for *Him* (Jesus)—that is, trying to get Jesus to apply the Word indiscriminately. He was seeking to get Jesus to apply power without being connected to the Throne Room protocol to own and guide the Scripture, instead of Scripture guiding and owning Him (to prove what was already established, to submit to someone who is suggesting a direction who should never be submitted to in anything, much less a direction quoting the Word).

Jesus would have been obeying the devil out of the direction in the suggestion. For us, it is using God, expecting Him to obey us, without a relationship. We do that a lot in the Body with the mentality that, "if we build it (ministry), they will come." We cannot use God's power for our own personal benefit on our own terms (including our ministry). Power comes from the Throne, and shows up in submission to it—in a flow from Heaven, not a generic declaration of words only based in assuming, not hearing.

The third deception was intended to get Jesus to believe that He did not already own all that the enemy was offering Him. That He was not the Son of the

Inheritance, but had gained his position thus far through the path out of Adam and Eve. The enemy was offering up for belief that the only way Jesus could get the kingdom back was through the worship of him (lucifer). He was tempting Jesus to compromise His worship in order to have fame and fortune, or inherit without paying the price. Jesus chose to sacrifice all that and protect His relationship with the Father.

> *Again, the devil taketh him up into an exceeding high mountain, and sheweth him all the kingdoms of the world, and the glory of them; And saith unto him, All these things will I give thee, if thou wilt fall down and worship me. Then saith Jesus unto him, Get thee hence, Satan: for it is written, Thou shalt worship the Lord thy God, and him only shalt thou serve. Then the devil leaveth him, and, behold, angels came and ministered unto him (Matt 4:8-11).*

There are so many times in Scripture where people were led astray by pride or lust. Saul, for example, offered up a sacrifice because the prophet was late. He acted in the pride of being the *king* while overstepping his boundaries because he was not the *priest.*

David is another example of how lust, and not staying hungry for the next set of adventures the Father had for him, changed his legacy. On the day he did not go to battle, the enemy set him up with the Bathsheba incident. We must realize that Adam and Eve lived in a paradise until the fall, then it became a war zone—for them, and for all humanity afterward.

Two forces are at war with each other, with humanity being the prize. There is the genuine experience with God, and because of it, the adversary has to counter with an imitation, or false experience. The adversary cannot create. Until he sees the real, he does not know how to counterfeit it. Once he sees God's real, he makes his offers of false.

A last thought on true and false visions: The vessel must have a pure heart. Seeing in the Spirit is all based upon the heart. We are talking about moving in the Spirit. There is a fine line between light and dark--we stay in the light as long as we stay connected to the Vine, or Jesus. (Jesus said, *I am the vine, you are the branches...*) He must be the center of our hearts. We do this by staying in a posture of humility and repentance. God resists the proud, and He gives grace to the humble. Just as satan has tempted and stolen throughout history, we can be sure he will test us as well.

There came a day for me when I discerned the enemy was trying to steal my gift. How did I know that? I discerned his subtle work through pride, as he offered to take me to places that were not ordained by the Lord. This was the curiosity to reach out into soulish power (which is what psychics and worldly, ungodly people do to have power without God). But, *a little leaven will leaven the whole lump (Gal 5:9)*. That little compromise would make the gift impure. The moment I had this subtle thought, immediately I knew I was under attack. The thief was coming to steal what the Lord had given. It was a great lesson to me that we have to learn to be alert at all times, and sensitive to what is the Lord, and what is *not* the Lord. I immediately took this temptation to Him and I began to repent for any pride or self-exaltation, and any open doors I had permitted. I let the Lord examine my heart. I ran to the feet of Jesus and stayed close to Him as the attack passed. I remembered this encounter, and I knew it was training ground. I needed to stay alert and on guard at all times. Purity is the key, and staying close to Jesus is the safest place to be. Hearing and obeying His voice is this place of safety. This experience left an imprint on my heart of the importance of always watching for the Lord. I believe the Lord was training me to be pure.

> *Be sober, be vigilant; because your adversary the devil, as a roaring lion, walketh about, seeking whom he may devour (1 Peter 5:8):*

God's visions give instruction and comfort. They lead us into peace, not false hope and empty promises. Many times the Lord will show me the future. He wants me to pray through to Him and change the outcome.

We need to get people activated to see in the spirit because each of us sees a part of the puzzle piece that the Lord has planned for His Church. I believe God does it that way because He wants us to need each other and realize we are not independent of one another. He wants us to not be threatened by our brothers and sisters in Christ but to celebrate, support, help, and exhort; thereby, encouraging them to go to higher heights in the Lord. He wants us to be a team, built up in unity and harmony for both the maturing of the Body and as a witness to the world. This harmony not only helps the Body function as it should, it also provides regular "course correction," and keeps us in alignment with God and each other.

When our hearts are healed and whole, we are able to hear the Lord with clarity because we are not protecting our turf or ourselves. We are in a position to build His Kingdom instead of ours. As believers, we are part of His Kingdom, but there is only one focus in our kingdom, and that is us. We must not be blind, but be able to see and hear—having all five senses activated, not shutting down out of woundedness and fear. In order to see in the spirit or hear from the Lord, we must always be open to what He is saying. We must not be "for" or "against" any situation in and of itself.

> *Joshua looked, and, behold, there was a man over against him with his sword drawn in his hand: and Joshua went unto him, and said unto him, Art thou for us, or for our adversaries? And he said, Nay; but as prince of the host of Jehovah am I now come. And Joshua fell on his face to the earth, and did worship, and said unto him, What saith my lord unto his servant? And the prince of Jehovah's host said unto Joshua, Put off thy shoe from off thy foot; for the place whereon thou standest is holy. And Joshua did so (Josh 5:13-15 ASV).*

In this scripture, we see that the posture of the angel is to bring forth the will of the Lord in the situation. He did not come to do his own thing for Joshua out of his position as a prince of God, but he came to carry out the orders of the Supreme King Jehovah. I have seen this posture many times on angels. I have seen "their set will" that will only move under the direction of the King of the Universe. I have learned this from watching them. There is a complete obedience to the King. I have longed for this attitude in my heart that I would be neither for nor against anyone, but instead for the Lord alone, and His will done in the earth.

So, too, we all must be for the Lord and Him alone. In order to see and hear accurately, we need to let go of our opinions and shortsighted thinking. If we do this, we will be able to hear the Father's heart. We must always remember that He is the Leader, and we are the followers.

I believe the Lord is going to show many people supernatural things. They will begin to have more and more heavenly encounters. We must believe God.

We must believe that God is greater than the power of the enemy to deceive us. The character of Jesus has been lacking in the church; therefore, we must keep our character pure. There are so few of God's people moving in the gifts today that we make an idol of those who do. But if we all take our rightful places and allow God's gifts to operate through each of us, the gifts will become the norm in the Body of Christ instead of the spectator sport it has sadly become.

We need to be so exercised in the spirit, so accustomed to seeing, hearing, tasting, touching, and smelling in the spirit, that we will no longer be impressed or fooled by the flesh. We will look for integrity and strong moral character in those operating in the gifts. The Lord wants to know us intimately. In that intimacy we will develop His character, and we will know and embrace the ways of God.

> *Many will say to me in that day, Lord, Lord, did we not prophesy by thy name, and by thy name cast our demons, and by thy name do many mighty works? And then will I profess unto them, I never knew you: depart from me, ye that work iniquity (Matt 7:22-23 ASV).*

> *"Write this letter to the angel of the church in Sardis. This is the message from the one who has the sevenfold Spirit of God and the seven stars: "I know all the things you do, and that you have a reputation for being alive—but you are dead. Now wake up! Strengthen what little remains, for even what is left is at the point of death. Your deeds are far from right in the sight of God. Go back to what you heard and believed at first; hold to it firmly and turn to me again. Unless you do, I will come upon you suddenly, as unexpected as a thief. "Yet even in Sardis there are some who have not soiled their garments with evil deeds. They will walk with me in white, for they are worthy. All who are victorious will be clothed in white. I will never erase their names from the Book of Life, but I will announce before my Father and his angels that they are mine. Anyone who is willing to hear should listen to the Spirit and understand what the Spirit is saying to the churches (Rev 3:1-6).*

These two scriptures speak of moral character being very important. The first passage, and part of the second, speaks of those who are gifted, yet their deeds were evil. They did not know the Lord intimately, neither did they have the voice of the Lord in them. The second part was about those who kept their garments clean, making sure the work that was done in the name of the Lord was pure and clean. There should not be any liars or deceivers in the Lord's house. We need to restore integrity and stop preserving our life and ministry at all costs. The Lord is watching (Rev 3:1). He knows all the things that we do. We need to walk with Him with that thought always before us, and have complete integrity and moral character.

Another important aspect of the seer gift is that sometimes all five of our senses are engaged. Not only will you see, but also you may feel (emotionally as well as physically), smell, taste, and hear. Your soul and spirit are acutely alert. That is why you may not be able to express everything that you are "seeing," because what you are seeing is not just physical sight, it is a cornucopia of senses. The heavenly is eternal; it is infinite. We must understand that everything that comes from the Lord is Heaven brought down to us. The Word of God came from Heaven's perspective. Jesus said, *I am the bread, which came down from Heaven (John 6:41 KJV).* As you meditate on what God has shown you, He will give you revelation after revelation after revelation. Even years later, the vision will be just as fresh as when you first had it. All you have to do is think about it and begin to meditate on it, and you will be right back in the sensation of the vision with new insight.

One day I asked the Lord about my gift. He explained that part of my gift is to call forth what I see from its spiritual form to its natural form. I also see what is happening around me. I see victory and encouragement, hope, love, joy, and giving in the life of believers. I see what the Spirit is doing at the moment over His people, and I see strategies of the enemy over people.

The Lord once showed me a picture of the Body of Christ and how it functioned. I saw the Body of Christ as puzzle pieces lying flat all around in a horizontal position. Jesus was standing vertical over the puzzle pieces. Each puzzle piece had a small part of Jesus on it. The pieces seemed to vibrate with the presence of the Lord, but they needed to be shaped and formed in order to fit together. Once the pieces were shaped and came together, they made a complete picture of Jesus. Some of the pieces were to be a part of the five-fold ministry. These pieces were shaped into a supportive form. Once they were complete, these pieces moved underneath the others and became a support system for the picture of Jesus.

Each puzzle piece needed the other so that the picture would be complete and powerful. As each piece joined together, the vibrations became stronger. They moved like one man, with a powerful sense of purpose. The picture of Jesus became more complete with its support systems in place. There was no big "I" or little "you." The only One Who was standing vertical was Jesus; the only One Who was seen was Jesus. If a puzzle piece would not yield to the shaping of the Father, if it got bitter and would not forgive, I saw it being placed on a shelf next to others like it. They continued to vibrate with His presence, but there was nothing for them to do. The point was for the puzzle piece to be shaped, then be joined together as the Father willed it. After a time of sitting on the shelf and unwillingness to turn from the unforgiving spirit or other obstacle to unity, the puzzle piece stopped vibrating and the picture seemed to disappear. I understood from the vision that Jesus wants to use all of us to lift Him up and He will do the work through us.

I also see angels. It is strange to me that this part of a believer's walk is viewed so controversially, as Scripture is filled with everyday people who saw angels. The Angel of the Lord appears 180 times in the Bible. One example is found in Genesis 16:7-8:

> *"Now the angel of the Lord found her by a spring of water in the wilderness, by the spring on the way to Shur. He said, 'Hagar, Sarai's maid, where have you come from and where are you going?' And she said, 'I am fleeing from the presence of my mistress Sarai'" (Gen 16:7-8 NASB).*

As we see, Hagar was a simple maid, yet her seed (which was the seed of Abraham) was important to the plan of God, and the Father sent His angel to give her direction and counsel.

I have always seen random things concerning my life. From time to time, the Lord will have me intercede for things that would affect other nations. I remember once when I was folding clothes in my early 20's, I heard a man on television speak about Christians who were being persecuted in Russia. As he was talking, I was judging him and saying to myself, "He is a fake." Suddenly, in the middle of my judging, I was in the air over Russia and I could see people being persecuted. I felt like they were my family members! I began to cry. It was such a heartrending cry that it came out of the depths of my being. Intercession fell on me out of nowhere. When the vision was over, I was not only surprised at the vision but at the overwhelming emotion I felt during the vision.

Later, I was watching the 700 Club, where host Pat Robertson was interviewing Christians who had come out of Russia. The year was 1974. A young girl and her parents were on the show, and Pat had the young girl pray. She was filled with the Spirit of God and prayed like a seasoned warrior. I knew these were some of the people God had me come into agreement with during that vision in Russia.

It is difficult to relate visions to others in their fullness because of the five senses that are involved and because a vision is spiritual. If a person is only listening with his mind, he will interpret the vision from an earthly or mental perspective and usually miss what the Lord is saying. We are often like Daniel. When he saw the end of the age, he was disturbed by what he "saw." He could feel the pain and see the turmoil. Yet, he could not put into words all that he was shown. This is what happens to those who see in the spirit. It is like describing a room. You focus more on the centerpiece of the room, or the main thought, than on something that is in your peripheral vision. How well you are able to put the picture into words depends on how detailed you are in your description. So, have grace for those who see in the spirit; they are conveying to you the sense of what they see. Some will be able to articulate what they are seeing better than others, but that does not take away from the purpose or intent of the message. As we support one another in our gifts and anointings, we will find the fear of man decreasing, which will enable a greater freedom for all to see and hear the Word of the Lord.

I, personally, see similarly as some of the characters in the Bible, such as Ezekiel, Isaiah, Elijah, etc. in the visions God gave them. I have had dreams like Joseph, when the Lord was showing him the future. The visions God gives me are sometimes glimpses of actual events. I once saw my youngest son at a party. He was in the middle of the floor, showing off, dancing and spinning. His brother later told me that my youngest son truly was showing off, dancing in the middle of the floor during that exact time. It was just as the Lord had shown me.

I do not search after these visions. They just come before my sight and I see whatever the Spirit of God wants to show me. When I see the pictures, I often don't understand the full interpretation, so I am left with questions. As I think about the vision and inquire of the Lord, He gives me more insight. If someone asks me questions about a vision, I am able to bring forth more details.

It seems as if the seer gift allows me to see the future, past, or present. It's difficult to describe, but picture taking a string and placing it at the center of your being and stretching it out into eternity as you look all along the string. The Spirit of God leads me to see segments of time. Sometimes, I am looking days into the future. At other times, I am looking ten years back, five years before, then back two years. At times, I will see the beginning of a thing that is starting to happen in God's church. At other times, He will show me the end of time. Whatever the Father wants me to see is what I see. It doesn't seem to come in any order; but He has told me to make sure I date everything I see. I think the Lord is building and strengthening my spirit-man so I can go where He is going and have an understanding from His vantage point.

There is one more point I want to make about seeing and hearing in the spirit. Heaven is filled with sights and sounds. Seeing in the Spirit is not like a silent movie—it is how we can recognize the true from the false. The sound provokes feelings of peace and rest when it is from the Lord. You feel and sense eternity. You sense His purpose and His will. I have heard of people who have gone to heaven or seen the Lord and the sense they describe is always one of peace. It's like a recognizing of a piece of us that had been lost in the garden, which I think is glorious beyond words. I believe it is like rediscovering part of the original design.

So Heaven is not only about sight, but Heaven has a sound. Those who hear Heaven's sound recognize it, for it is pure. It is like a homing beacon built within our DNA. It is a tuning fork that aligns our lives and everything around us with God. Some music that is pure carries this sound. That is why we love music, and why it is a unifier and a bridge-builder. Certain sounds in music remind us of the sound that dwells within. Here are some scriptural sounds from eternity:

Whoever does not love does not know God, because God is love (1 John 4:8).

The Father's love pouring out of us has a sound that brings peace. It also emanates out of the character of the one that walks with the Lord. We all discern this character even though we might not know how to put words to what we sense. We do this by avoidance if the person carries a negative spirit, or we can be drawn into the sense of peace an individual might carry. These scriptures clearly cover seeing and hearing at the same time:

> *On the Lord's Day I was in the Spirit, and I heard behind me a loud voice like a trumpet…His feet were like bronze glowing in a furnace, and his voice was like the sound of rushing waters (Rev 1:10, 15).*

> *As I watched, I heard an eagle that was flying in midair call out in a loud voice: "Woe! Woe! Woe to the inhabitants of the earth, because of the trumpet blasts about to be sounded by the other three angels!" (Rev 8:13 NIV).*

Heaven's sound can be heard in the voices of those who have seen into the heavenly realm. Most are aware that a "seer" can see into the heavenlies, but some are unaware that Heaven has a glorious sound of peace and love that is imparted to those who see and hear. That is why, once you have visited the heavenlies, there will be a sound coming forth as you describe heavenly experiences. For example, there was a lady who had been burned who was being interviewed on a news program. She was telling how she was helped out of a burning plane by an angel. The moment she spoke, I could hear Heaven's sound in her voice; and before she finished her story, I knew that God had saved her and that she had seen into the heavenlies. Even though she had been disfigured and had gone through a traumatic experience, she was at peace. Heaven's eternal sound carries peace and gives peace to those who have ears to hear.

Beyond the Veil includes heavenly visions as well as earthly visions. If I did not have the impartation of the heavenly visions, I could not properly interpret the earthly visions. I would be taking the earthly to the heavenlies, but not bringing the heavenlies back down to earth. You will see as you read my story that as I am seeing into the heavenlies, my natural, unregenerated mind is thinking from an earthly perspective while my regenerated spirit is tuned into the heavenly realm.

> *As the heavens are higher than the earth, so are my ways higher than your ways and my thoughts than your thoughts (Isaiah 55:9 NIV),*

When we look at this natural world, we can sometimes miss the beauty that God has created, even though it is everywhere. If we take a moment to really look at the sky, the heavens—or even a simple flower—we will begin to see God and His glory! One day the Lord spoke to me and asked, "Have you noticed my clouds and the miracle that lies within them?" The clouds look so light and fluffy. It's as if we can hold them in the palms of our hands. If the clouds get low to the ground, we can hide in their fog. We can fly through them; yet, they can be heavy with tons of water and so violent that they will destroy cities and towns in seconds. What an awesome miracle we look at every day without really noticing the greatness of our God. Scripture says, "*The heavens declare the glory of God; and the firmament sheweth his handiwork*" *(Psalm 19:1)*. He is all around us with great wonders.

It is amazing how we have sights and sounds all around us, yet we can go day after day without seeing or hearing them. Those who are willing can look beyond what is going on with their natural senses and listen with their hearts. But in order to do this, we must quiet ourselves from all the noise and all the distractions of this life. When there is stillness within and without, we can hear Heaven's true sound. Truth is all around us. God's Truth, which is the Holy Spirit, discloses Jesus and His glory to His beloved children.

> *...the Spirit of truth. The world cannot accept him, because it neither sees him nor knows him. But you know him, for he lives with you and will be in you (John 14:17).*

Won't you still your soul and your body long enough to hear the glorious sounds of Heaven? My personal journaling in Beyond the Veil is my story of learning to be still in His presence so that He could show me His glorious Kingdom. I hope that—if you are not already at the same place—you, too, may discover the glorious sounds and truths of Heaven that are all around us.

He who has an ear, let him hear what the Spirit says to the churches
(Rev 2:7 NASB).

The purpose of this book is two-fold. First, I was simply obedient to the Lord in translating some of the many experiences He has given me to paper. Part of my husband's and my journey is to understand where God has brought us from, so we can learn from our mistakes, rejoice in the victories, and go from glory to glory.

We believe in impartation and in equipping the saints, so this book is also designed to stir and build up the seer gift in *you*. To this end, you will find that throughout the book I have added two types of "teaching" boxes: Steps of Understanding (interpretation of the dream or vision immediately before the box), and Kingdom Keys (principles and keys to going deeper in the things of God).   Maybe you are at the beginning of your schooling in the spirit realm, or maybe you are already a seasoned believer but desiring to be activated in your giftings in an even greater way. Wherever you are in your own journey, I pray that you will find confirmation, revelation, and encouragement in these pages, and that you will allow the Holy Spirit to speak to you through them to take your spiritual gifts to the next level.

Prologue:

Life on the Other Side

It was a hot summer day in July 1964, around 1 PM, when suddenly there was a knock on our door. My mother answered it to find an elderly lady standing there in a grey wig. She was a slender woman, with a beaming face and a heart filled with the love of God. Mom and I had just finished lunch and were talking at the kitchen table when our visitor arrived. This day is burned into my memory, because it was the day that I had planned to do something that would have ruined the rest of my life.

I remember contemplating most of the day how I would kill a certain person who was living with us. This person had damaged our family's emotions to a breaking point; we were terrorized by his behavior, and I had had enough. Age twelve and the oldest of seven children, I remember sweeping the floor and visualizing exactly how I would carry out what I had planned. It was in my heart, and was completely taking over my mind. I had been sitting and talking with my mother like everything was perfectly normal with me, all the while resolute in what I was going to do. And then came the knock that would change everything.

This sweet lady came into our home with a bounce in her step and a smile on her face, sharing with me and my mother the good news about a man named Jesus. We believed her, and instantly my life took a complete shift. For the first time in my 12 years, I felt loved, safe and protected.

Jesus became so real to me. I then began to remember things I had forgotten. One of the experiences that came back to me was when I was seven. I had been told to go to bed, but I was very afraid. I seemed to be fearful of everything. I was lying there sobbing as I stared out the window that faced my bed. As I cried in the dark, I was asking Jesus to help me. I do not know how I knew about Jesus, since my family was not religious. My mother never went to church, so I must have heard my grandfather talk about Jesus, because he often quoted the Word and spoke about Jesus only. He also belonged to a church that was part of the "Jesus only" movement. These may have been the seeds that the Lord had sown in my hearing.

I began to call on Jesus to help me. I was crying out with every ounce of my young, frightened heart. As I cried and stared at the window, suddenly Jesus appeared and came into my room, floating on a cloud. A feeling of perfect peace and comfort settled over me. He came up to me and placed His hand on my head, and said, "Sleep, my child." I immediately fell into a sweet, deep sleep. I awoke the next morning and excitedly told my mother, but she told me to stop lying, so in disappointment and confusion I retreated into myself because I believed my mother over what I had seen with my own eyes. But I never forgot this vision. It was burned into my heart. Years later, I would tell my mother about the visitation, and she then believed me. She did not remember her reply to me or the effect that it had had on me as a child, but I understood that she was learning just as I was. She went on to have many visitations from the Lord herself.

When I gave my heart to the Lord, this was the first vision that came back to me. I thought to myself, *"Did I actually get saved at that moment? Because He called me His child!"* He was taking care of my life to make sure I did not mess it up.

After receiving the Lord, we began going to the church where the lady was attending, which was housed in the Metropolitan Opera House in Philadelphia, known to all as "the Met." Thea Jones was the pastor. He was a faith healer who had stepped into the ministry when Jack Coe (a famous healing minister at the time) got cold feet and would not go out on stage when the healing service began. He had advertised that everyone who came in a wheelchair would leave walking if they came to the event.

That night, the church filled every one of its seats and overflow areas—10,000 people—and 300 people in wheelchairs showed up. Overwhelmed by the response, and possibly feeling he went too far in his confidence, Coe suddenly left and Thea Jones was there with a packed church and no guest speaker. Feeling that the people deserved to have someone pray for them, he went out and with simple integrity said, "In the name of Jesus, get up and walk!" All but three people stood up and walked out of their wheel chairs. This was the start of Thea Jones' ministry. From then on, he walked in a great healing gift from the Lord. City officials would come out to the healing meeting, and famous healing evangelists came through Philadelphia to hold services there. Everyone who was anyone in ministry in those days came to the Met.

By the time I started attending the church, this was all history, but it was still packed with members that were big on evangelism and preaching the full Gospel. I started going to the all night prayer meetings with my sister, who was two years younger than me. So at age 12 and 10, we would walk to church in the evenings and stay all night in prayer. Along with my mother, we grew up breathing the air of Heaven, watching the many miracles take place in Thea Jones' ministry as well as those who came through there to teach and walk in gifts of healing, deliverance and miracles. I saw blind eyes open. I saw people who were born deaf begin to hear. I saw the crippled walk. We lived in an atmosphere where things like this were not only possible, but normal.

I started having visitations from the Lord. As my mother and I prayed, the walls would turn from white to a pink. We would smell a sweet fragrance that would fill the room. I started reading where Jesus said, "The works that I do, you will do greater." I believed this word with all my heart. I began to pray for my friends, and they began to be healed. People were getting delivered from evil spirits. The Holy Spirit was moving greatly.

One day, we were told about a tent meeting that was happening in Philadelphia. It was called Miracles, Signs, and Wonders, and was being held by a minister by the name of A.A. Allen. My mother took me and a few of her friends to the meeting. The tent was packed every night with people coming from all the surrounding areas of Delaware, New Jersey, and Pennsylvania, and even New York and Washington.

God's presence was there with power, starting with Gene Martin, who led the choir and would sing until God's presence filled the place. He would walk up and down the aisles praising the Lord with such a fire that no one could stay sitting in their seats for very long.

On one of the days he was singing, I began to watch the people around me dancing in the spirit (that is what they did in those days when they felt God's presence). I thought I would join in and mimic some of them. They were dancing in the spirit so I pretended I was doing the same. Suddenly, my little "game" fell away as the true spirit of God came over me and I was shocked to find myself begin to shake. His presence filled my little body. He was all over me, and I began to jump straight up and down. My mother looked at me, and the people around me stared as I was overwhelmed by His presence. I thought, *Oh my God. I was just playing, but now this is REAL!*

I have often thought of that moment, how God came when I was not expecting Him. I thought I would play with God and He came and played with me. How awesome our God is!

A.A. Allen came yearly to Philadelphia. We saw every miracle you can think of. We saw the blind see, the lame walk, cancers healed, the deaf hear, legs grow out—it was like walking with Jesus during His days on the earth to me. It was the Bible. I read what Jesus did, and the meetings I went to demonstrated it before my eyes. So this was normal Christianity for me.

I had joined the choir by now, and was becoming acquainted with the minister's children who all attended the meetings with their parents. I went backstage once, and one of the minister's sons had gotten a new motor bike that he was showing off to us kids. His name was Bobby, and his father was R.W. Schambach, who went on to build a miracle ministry as well.

Later that day, I was with some other kids in the sawdust while the meetings were going on. We had come for all the services, so I was playing when suddenly out of nowhere, A.A. Allen was walking through the tent. He had on cowboy boots, blue jeans and a cowboy hat. This was strange to me because I had only ever seen him on stage in a dress shirt and tie. He walked past us as we were playing, and he looked straight at me with his piercing eyes. He said, "Hi, little sweetie," and patted me on the head.

That night I sang in the choir; I was on the front row because I was small. A.A. Allen was ministering on "Race Rioting in America," and there were a couple thousand people in the tent. He was a fiery preacher, walking up and down the stage, talking of this race riot that would take place.

Suddenly in the middle of his message, he turned around, pointed at me and shouted, "They would not know whether to shoot her or not!" I was completely shocked that a minister would do that to a child. It was especially traumatic since I was a typical young teen who was horrified by any type of embarrassment. I had long released the pain of the moment, but thought about the significance of it many times, wondering what it all meant (A.A. Allen laying hands on my head and then that night calling me out to everyone). I now believe it is highly possible that the Lord imparted something to me when Allen laid his hands on my head. He knew God had just moved, and was meditating on me when he addressed me from the pulpit. I myself have had this experience, where God was moving by His Spirit through my hands without any prior knowledge, and the person was unaware. If so, an impartation from A.A. Allen went to me from Father God, per His plan, over my life.

The last night (which was the last service A.A. Allen ever preached in Philadelphia), they were talking about creating a place called Miracle Valley, where people could go for prayer and miracles. I would often remember those days, and was blessed by what I saw and learned.

I went on to get further involved at the Met, and at 15 I joined the evangelism team, taking tracts to the center of downtown Philadelphia every day after school. There is an open square at city hall, with an entrance to the city from each direction. Everyone coming in converges on this spot. I would stand there and give out all the tracts I had in my backpack, which was usually about 100. I took my job seriously. Anytime I saw someone throw one away, I would dig it out of the trash and give it to them again.

After I finished handing out my tracts for the day, I would go up into the tower that was on top of city hall. There was a statue of Benjamin Franklin over the tower where tourists could go and see the entire city of Philadelphia. I would go up and pray for the city. I'd pray on each side of the tower—north, south, east and west. I prayed for the Lord to move on the city and save the people, whatever the Lord led me to pray. This was my ritual every day after school, unless the weather was bad.

Years later, I met my husband Seymour. He worked for Thea Jones' eldest son in Greenwood, SC but had come up north to run a drug rehab center they were planning to establish. The program was never developed, so Seymour wound up being the assistant to Thea Jones. He made all the arrangements for Thea's media outlets on 300 TV stations and many radio stations. I began to travel with Thea as well, because of my relationship to Seymour. It was big ministry at its height. We learned all the things *not* to do in the house of God. Like Eli the priest, who indulged his sons in Scripture, many things were permitted to go on in the ministry. The people were not governed or pastored, which opened the door for anyone with ambition or bitter jealousy to rule the church. Surely we saw this scripture manifested in this ministry:

> *But if you have bitter jealousy and selfish ambition in your heart, do not be arrogant and so lie against the truth. This wisdom is not that which comes down from above, but is earthly, natural, demonic. For where jealousy and selfish ambition exist, there is disorder and every evil thing (James 3:14-16).*

At the height of these things, the Lord spoke to Seymour and me to leave and never return. Thea never forgot Seymour; we heard he would often speak of him. He asked his son to contact Seymour to pray when he fell ill. The Lord spoke to Seymour that he would not recover, and he did not. Thea died of a hip operation and went home to be with the Lord.

An associate of Thea's was left with the huge Met building which covered an entire city block, and she asked Seymour to come and take over the ministry. We could have sold the building for millions of dollars and done extremely well financially. But we had long ago decided to obey the Lord, and He had said, *"Never return to that place."* We, of course, obeyed.

We later went to a Freda Lindsay meeting. She had taken over her husband Gordon's ministry, Christ for the Nations, after his death. He had also moved with God in great faith. Freda had a college that raised up young people in the Lord.

The Lord was giving us a new vision. As Freda ministered, I suddenly went into an open vision. I saw my house on fire. I walked up to the door and put my hand in the fire and pulled it back out. It was blistered. I then put my hand back into the fire and it came out whole. I walked into the fire through the doorway, where I got soot all over my face and clothes. I went back into the fire and I was made clean.

I came out of the vision when we had a break, and immediately called home to see if my house was ok. All was well. After I came back I went into another vision. I saw a great whirlwind that went up to the heavens. It was upside down, so that the narrow part of the whirlwind was in the heavens and the wide part was on the earth. There was a door at the bottom and Jesus was standing at the door, holding the wind back like a curtain. I looked into the funnel and it had a spiral stairway that went upward, only there was a landing every eight stairs—a landing, eight stairs, then another landing and another eight stairs, and so on. This continued all the way up until it got to the top, where the stairs were fewer and the landings no longer were there. Inside the whirlwind it was golden and beautiful with a deep stillness, even though outside it was whirling as a mighty wind. Jesus looked at me and said, "This is your ministry." I stepped in, and He sealed the door behind me.

I knew the meaning was that I would go through great testing and fiery trials. I would also be cleaned of many things, hence my house of fire. My life was the house. After the testing was over I would move into a new phase in my life where there would be periods of time that I would begin pulling things down from Heaven into Earth. Jesus said, "…as it is in Heaven, let it be in Earth." The steps were a measurement of time in my life. It would happen, then there would be a lull, hence the landings. Toward the end of the whirlwind, I would go straight up with no stopping, just a pouring out of what the Lord wanted.

After this I came out of the vision. Freda had begun to pray before the Lord. Suddenly she called Seymour and spoke over him, saying he would be greatly used by God; that if he could count the stars of the heaven then he would be able to count the amount of souls the Lord would give him. After saying this she marveled that these words came out of her mouth. Seymour and I hid these visions and words in our heart, wondering what it all meant.

We went on to get involved in radio ministry and then the Lord led us to a group that started most of the apostle movement that has swept the world. We were part of the young lions that joined this movement. They had a powerful movement initially, and may they be found in the LORD when the Church in the earth tries the apostles and finds that they are not (Rev. 2:2).

A WORD FROM THE AUTHOR

I must say, the Lord has been merciful to me so many times. When he showed me that I needed to walk through whatever He put before me and love unconditionally, I sought His Face until He endued me with His heart of love. When I needed to believe, He graciously walked me through my own weakness, my faithlessness and my lack of understand of His ways, until NOW I am walking by faith.

Lastly, there were times when I was definitely in a religious spirit and didn't recognize it. Oh, my Father is so kind, He gently took me by the hand and taught me. All these things are only a few examples of what was in front of me when I started my journey through the veil. May you also have a great journey into His purifying fire until He says, Well done! Trust me, the journey is worth it all..

Chapter 1

Going Beyond the Veil

Let's go on a journey beyond the veil of our natural understanding, our natural minds. God has a way of speaking that is not to our minds, but to our spirits. He wants us to see in the spirit by training us to use our spiritual eyes. He causes our spiritual eyes to see pictures. In those pictures He not only gives us great and marvelous revelation about Himself but also about the world and us.

For example, the Father showed Daniel future events that would affect a generation not yet born.

While I was contemplating the horns, behold, another horn, a little one, came up among them, and three of the first horns were pulled out by the roots before it, and behold, this horn possessed eyes like the eyes of a man and a mouth uttering great boasts. 12:8: And I heard, but I understood not: then said I, O my lord, what shall be the issue of these things? And he said, Go thy way, Daniel; for the words are shut up and sealed till the time of the end. Many shall purify themselves, and make themselves white, and be refined; but the wicked shall do wickedly; and none of the wicked shall understand; but they that are wise shall understand (Dan 7:8 & 12:8-10 NASB).

We will enter this journey with spiritual eyes and explore some of the visions given to me for this appointed time in history. While you will understand most of the visions, at times some of them may be hard to interpret because of the difficulty of communicating pictures into words. I am seeing pictures of God's ways in action. In other words, I was seeing natural things in a "Pictionary" form.

Daniel saw the future we are living in today. He also saw the key ingredient to understanding and perceiving the revelations that the Lord would reveal to His people. It was that they cleansed themselves. It is the cleansing and the refining that causes the eyes to see and the ear to hear. Jesus made it clear in the Beatitudes when he said, "Blessed are the pure in heart, for they shall see God." Wickedness causes the heart to be blinded from the things of God, but the pure will understand the things of God.

During a vision, my whole being is engaged. I actually feel the emotions and hear the sounds along with the pictures, whether it is joy, peace, sadness, or dread. Daniel was an example of a seer experiencing emotions along with a vision God gave him.

> *So I was left there all alone to see this amazing vision. My strength left me, my face grew deathly pale, and I felt very weak (Dan 10:8 NLT).*

Also, I have learned that with these visions there is an impartation that takes place. Afterwards, my life is lined up more with the ways of God, which brings much strength. God wants us to be synchronized with Him. By showing us what Heaven is doing, He empowers us to come into agreement with the plan He has had for us from the beginning of time. It is critical to be able to see what Heaven is doing, so that if there is anything out of alignment, we can correct it. Through God's word pictures, an imprint from Heaven is left on our spirit man, and we are changed—never to be the same! Through these visions, I began to realize the awesomeness and the overwhelming greatness of God and how we are all born with a purpose. I have known this mentally, but it's now become a reality stamped on my spirit man.

There are many in Scripture whose lives were used for God's purposes. One of them was Job. When we are suffering, we often think of him. Another is Stephen. As a new Christian, he was martyred to show forth God's glories. Even though he had a short ministry, his testimony was so powerful that a seed was planted in Paul for him to become a mighty Christian and later write most of the New Testament.

The purpose of the beggar, Lazarus, is long remembered as Jesus used him in a parable in Luke 16:19. Daily, Lazarus sat by the rich man's gate. His life was used to ask, "Won't you have mercy on the poor?" The Lord sent a dog to lick his wounds to demonstrate mercy. In contrast, the rich man went in and out of his gate and never thought about the preciousness of Lazarus' life. The story would have been different had the rich man's heart softened toward Lazarus. At their deaths, the tables were turned. The rich man watched as Lazarus was being comforted and he suffered his eternal fate. God loved him so much that he sent His willing servant to suffer and be a sign to the unrighteous man.

This book may help you see that your life was meant for something far beyond what you can now understand, and that your life touches others for His perfect, ultimate plan. As I take you on this journey, I will be giving you a record of the visions I have seen, and the dates that I have seen them. They are written in chronological order. I want your faith to be built up to know that we have a loving and giving Father whose heart is toward His children. I have seen that the Lord delights in giving us every spiritual gift. He wants us to know what He is doing in the affairs of men and in future events. He wants us to stand in the gap for people as well as nations. He wants us to turn the tide with our prayers and intercessions.

> *And I sought for a man among them, that should build up the wall, and stand in the gap before me for the land, that I should not destroy it; but I found none (Ezek 22:30 ASV).*

Approximately six months before the 9/11 attack in NYC, God gave me a vision[1] so that I could stand in the gap for the United States. I was walking through my living room when suddenly I was standing on the steps of the United States Capitol building in Washington, DC. I was on the left side of the steps looking to my right. The scene was surreal. I looked up and saw a gray, slow moving missile coming toward me. I knew it was going to hit the Capitol. I felt disbelief that anything like this could happen to the United States. I was full of terror, and could not believe what I was seeing; my mouth dropped, and my eyes were wide

---

[1] *See interpretation of vision on next page in "Steps of Understanding," which is the first of several boxes placed throughout this book to aid in "unpacking" the seer gift.*

open. I was unable to move—frozen on that spot! I could do nothing but watch this missile coming straight toward the capitol.

When I see a vision two or more times, I know God is revealing to me that the vision will come to pass if He does not change His mind and intervene. Throughout that week, I saw the same vision three times. Even though I was still in disbelief; I knew I was seeing something important, and I was troubled that it might happen. So I told my husband, Seymour, about the vision and asked him, "Do you think we could be attacked?" He simply said, "Pray, and ask God not to let it happen." I began to seek the Lord for His mercy to be over our nation.[2]

---

[2] *History tells us that Flight 93 crashed 15 minutes from Washington, DC. It is widely assumed the intended target was the U.S. Capitol. Even though some heroic lives were lost, many lives were saved because God intervened and had mercy on this nation.*

Chapter 2

The Writing in the Wind

Late in the year of 1989, I was in prayer and had a vision where I saw a dark wind storm blowing from the west to the east, moving across the United States. As I looked, I could see an old car through the debris. It was sitting in the storm with the wind whipping all around it. The vision reminded me of a scene from the movie, *The Grapes of Wrath*. There was nothing growing as far as the eye could see. Suddenly, a hand appeared that began to write a date in the wind. It was much like writing on a blackboard with your finger. As the finger wrote, the wind was dispersed forming the date, October 3, 1991. I wrote this date down but at the time I did not know what it meant.

When October 3rd came, I watched television to see if anything important was happening. The only thing of significance was Bill Clinton putting his hat in the ring to run against President George W. Bush for president of the United States. I thought to myself that this could be what I had seen in the vision. From history, we know he won the presidency.

In 1989 the phrase, "the perfect storm" became popular. A movie released in 2000 was called The Perfect Storm, about people who lost their lives as they were out fishing when a storm of historic proportions came upon them. I believe America has been, and is now, in a perfect storm. I believe that the vision I had is ongoing. The Clintons are very much a part of the governing of America past, present, and future. I am not saying they are the cause of what America is going through, but their lives are a mark of something different coming to our land. Clinton's presidency brought a wind of change—winds of change that are still blowing. It seems as though all that we were economically, socially, politically, and spiritually has blown away in the wind, and set the stage for what has come after.

This election year, America will choose whether she desires this change to be taken to the next level. We will be able to see where we are on God's timeline by what takes place in November. Never have the intercessors and prayer warriors been needed more to cry out of behalf of our nation; she is in deep distress, and she cannot rise up without them.

Steps of Understanding
(Interpretation):

In this vision about "The Writing in the Wind", the Lord was showing me future events of our country; that the United States would fall into great spiritual darkness, flowing from the west coast to the east coast. This darkness would create a barrenness—spiritually, economically, socially, and physically. The old car represented our spiritual inheritance and values that we have deemed old and worthless, no longer having any value in the heart of anyone that remembered them. The young did not value them because they were not born into an age of morality, and did know what it was like to fight for freedom or hold the line on integrity. The old ways have been abandoned and not passed on to this lustful, prideful, rebellious generation.

Chapter 3

Between Heaven and Earth

The War Against the Saints in Charleston

July 1990

After moving to Charleston, South Carolina, Seymour and I were at a prayer meeting with a church group in the inner city. I knew nothing of the area or the surrounding communities. As I prayed, I saw a vision of ships coming into the Charleston harbor. As they neared the shores, they shipwrecked, and I could see bodies all over the seashore. After seeing this vision, I prayed, "Lord, please don't let this happen to us."

Later, we met many people the Lord had sent to Charleston whose lives were shipwrecked. Before coming to Charleston, they were very successful in the work of the Lord. After coming, many marriages were destroyed and many had gone into poverty through uncommon circumstances. Inexplicably, people would go from perfect health to sickness. Many were discouraged and had a lack of trust in anyone or anything; therefore, there was disunity among those that God had sent to the city. Some even needed counseling and mental help. Everyone seemed to go into survival mode, doing anything to try to preserve life as they had known it.

We have also met those who are still standing despite the battles. They have done all to stand, and they are standing, though weary. They are hungry to see God move. They will not be put out of their places and are holding the line until

God shows up. This place is a true battlefield, but we know God has a plan. He is never defeated. We will stand and see the salvation of the Lord.

The Lord will send His people in areas to take ground. They must not be self-focused or money-focused. They are there to do the business of the King. There are rulers over cities that the Lord has sent His troops into. They are sent to be trained and learn how to stand against the adversity that they encounter. Many times, people don't understand that the Father is calling them to be His ambassadors and intercessors for that city. We also learned that you need not partake of the spirits over the region you live in. For example: The spirits over Charleston are pride, disunity, competition, fear of one another, etc. If the servants of God acted in this manner, they became ineffective. You must come in the opposite spirit in order to win the victory.

We have become so ministry-focused, rather than God's purpose-focused, that the moment we encounter a trial or a tribulation, we often drop the assignment like a hot potato, when the Lord is wanting us to be a territorially governing people. Because many have given up the territory due to the hardships, the enemy rules even where His people were sent to do the business of the King and to stand.

This is what we have seen in Charleston. Many came, and many went. The pattern was always the same: financial, relational, physical, and psychological ruin! The reason these things happened was the inability of the servants to understand the purposes of the testing. The Lord was seeking to build true warriors of the Kingdom, who would be able to stand under any circumstance. Theirs was to listen to the Lord and obey Him, resting in whatever circumstance they were found in. The Lord wanted His ambassadors to pray through until the victory came and the city was won for the glory of God. But instead of faith being built into the heart, many became afraid, and did not trust the Lord for their victory. Instead, they sought out a fast victory somewhere else that was not their assignment.

I remember a story told to us by a very good friend. He spoke of a minister who had built a huge church with thousands of members. Anyone looking at him would have called him a success. He told my friend that the Lord actually had called him to India to be a missionary. He did it for a while, but did not like the hardship so he came home and started a church and built it successfully (again, in the world's eyes). The Lord had called Him to the job that He wanted him to do, which was working in India. This man chose his own way, and the ministry he wanted for himself. What will happen when He stands before God without the souls of India in his hands? This was his assignment, and nothing else. He knew his assignment, and refused to do it. He took his natural skills of management and put them to work for himself to perform *his* will and not the will of God. Unfortunately, many have taken this route, without thinking of the consequences.

Into the Heavens
1994

I was listening to worship music and resting in the Lord in prayer one day. A male vocalist was playing a guitar and singing, "The Lord Is My Shepherd." The music was gentle and sweet to my soul. Suddenly, I saw a beautiful city. It was square, and pure white and gold. I was at the bottom of a soft, sloping hill looking up at this city. The grass was a beautiful, vibrant green and seemed to be alive. I had the sense that everyone in the city knew me, and somehow I knew them. It seemed that everyone had one heart and one spirit. Then I noticed a pool of water at the bottom of the hill where I was standing. Suddenly, I was in the pool looking up at the city and I was under the water, breathing. This was amazing to me because I was breathing living water. I knew I was going to be a part of this city.

The city was the Kingdom of God. I was seeing God's beautiful place that He has prepared for those that love Him. The heavens had opened before me, and God was preparing me for more visits to this city. I was being prepared to see even greater things. It all started with being washed in the pool of water at the foot of the hill of the Kingdom of God.

Matthew 11:27 tells us, *All things have been committed to me by my Father. No one knows the Son except the Father, and no one knows the Father except the Son and those to whom the Son chooses to reveal him (NIV)*. I believe I was going through a type of baptism before I could enter the Kingdom of God so that I could see much clearer. I was being washed from the inside out.

Sometimes, we don't acknowledge how holy our God is and how much washing away of the flesh there needs to be. The Holy Spirit was taking me on a journey to a deeper revelation of the ways of the Father. I needed to learn how to stay in a place of repentance. I needed to take my little sins and faults to Him, learn to be forgiven and to forgive others, and have a heart that would be in a state of continuous change until Jesus "be fully formed in me." Learning to walk in His ways is so glorious. Everything the Lord does brings joy and peace.

There is an invisible kingdom of light all around us. Even though it is invisible, it is more real than what we see with our natural eyes. There are forces beyond our ability that guide and shape our destiny. We can rest, that God is in control. As we pray, we can be led by God's presence and shaped by Him if we will obey Him. We have a free will to let the Kingdom of light guide us. Precious Lord Holy Spirit does this leading and guiding.

> *While we look not at the things which are seen, but at the things which are not seen; for the things which are seen are temporal, but the things which are not seen are eternal (2 Cor 4:18 NASB).*

There are many baptisms in Scripture.[3] As the children of Israel went through the Red Sea, they were baptized into a new beginning. They had to be tried and tested in that new beginning so that they might see their own hearts. In order to come fully into the new place the Lord had prepared for them, they had to release the old, and believe the Father fully for the new life they were being given. Your faith will go through a baptism of fire to see what you really believe and what is in the heart of each person that claims they believe in God. Faith is what stands on the ground with the Father.

John the Baptist was baptizing those who believed and were looking for the Hope of Israel, which was Jesus the Messiah. If they could believe, they could step into that hope. The Pharisees who refused to believe John's baptism, the forerunner of Jesus the Messiah, did not recognize or believe Jesus when he

---

[3] *I noticed each time I would go to Heaven there would be a type of baptism, whether it be water, oil or fire, etc. These baptisms each ushered in a change in me.*

came. They did not cross over into the new thing. Even though the way was made for them, they would not believe (John addressed the few that did show up at the Jordan, exposing their wrong motives). Their system was built around the old baptism of Moses, and they chose their position and place in that system instead of this new way of relating to God. The Rabbinic leadership chose to be faithful to the system they had already learned to manipulate and corrupt, which brought deception and rejection of God's plan.

> *When all the people and the tax collectors heard this, they acknowledged God's justice, having been baptized with the baptism of John. But the Pharisees and the lawyers rejected God's purpose for themselves, not having been baptized by John (Luke 7:29-30).*

Another example of this baptism is found in Mark:

> *But Jesus said to them, "You don't know what you are asking. Are you able to drink the cup that I drink, and to be baptized with the baptism that I am baptized with?" They said to him, "We are able." Jesus said to them, "You shall indeed drink the cup that I drink, and you shall be baptized with the baptism that I am baptized with; (Mark 10:38, 39):*

From Heaven's point of view, you must go through a type of baptism to enter into the new place that the Lord has for His people. This baptism comes from Heaven and it comes to those that will believe. (John possessed the ability to impart the faith for the new wineskin. John was the new wineskin. Jesus was the New Wine. True faith is carving out a new wineskin today, especially among youthful hearts, and a new wine is coming.) Jesus was speaking of a baptism of death to bring about a new covenant and a new kingdom. He went through this baptism of death and we know that His disciples flowed in turn, each one dying so that the Kingdom could be birthed into being.

Another baptism is coming for the Church. It will be a baptism from Heaven. You will not be able to fake your way in this new baptism; this baptism has a sound. The simple and pure will walk through without any effort. You must rest in the Lord in order to enter in. Heaven is looking at the heart, not our efforts.

The key to this baptism is loving the Father and wanting Him more than anything—more than our intellect, relationships, ministry, fame, money or anything we hold dear to our hearts above Him.

That little spark of wanting the Father will bring us into this baptism. Religion is a wall against it. Just as the Pharisees had a wall against John the Baptist, so too, anyone with a religious heart will not be able to enter in. It will be impossible for them, for the way will be blocked to anyone who wants the Father on their terms. You must be willing to hear Him and obey Him.

This baptism will be one of "resting in the Lord" in the midst of great turmoil. This rest will bring peace in the midst of the storm. It will produce faith that will take us to a new place of seeing the Father and who He is. It will open our eyes to see into the heavens as never before, even as John saw in the book of Revelation. The faith of the ages will come down, and the glory of the Lord will cover many people. You don't have to be special or great, a minister, or renowned. You just have to want the Lord.

> *For the one who has entered His rest has himself also rested from his works, as God did from His. Therefore let us be diligent to enter that rest, so that no one will fall, through following the same example of disobedience (Heb 4:10-11).*

> *Therefore, just as the Holy Spirit says, "Today if you hear His voice, do not harden your hearts as when they provoked Me, as in the day of trial in the wilderness, where your fathers tried Me by testing Me, And saw My works for forty years. Therefore I was angry with this generation, And said, 'They always go astray in their heart, And they did not know My ways '; As I swore in My wrath, 'They shall not enter My rest'" (Heb 3:7-11)*

Chapter 4

The Forming of the Bride

Revival

June 1997

We went to a revival in Pensacola, FL. People came from all over the world to this mighty move of God, where He was touching people in miraculous ways. In a vision, I saw waterfalls in the sanctuary. At times, I would feel the sanctuary shake with the praises of God's people. I wanted so much for Jesus to fill me. I wanted to receive all that Jesus ordained for this revival.

On one occasion, the ministers who worked alongside one of the pastors were to go down the aisle praying for people. An announcement went out before they prayed that there would be no one prophesying over us; we were to stand in the aisle and someone would pray for us. Seymour and I stood in the aisle waiting. A minister came up to us and said, "Who are you?" We replied, "We are pastors of a church in Summerville, SC." He began to prophesy over us and said, "You are not called to restore the old. You are going to see (usher in) the new." He was saying the revival we were in was about restoring the holiness of God and a repentant heart, but there was something new coming to the Church, and we would be a part of this new thing birthed in the Kingdom. This pastor had gotten the lead minister of the revival out of jail and discipled him. Only he could have had the authority to move in the gifts of prophecy to us without violating the direction the pulpit had set through the head minister. After he laid hands on Seymour and me, I fell down under the weight of the glory of the Lord. I immediately went into an open vision. Seymour and I were standing in wedding attire at the pearly gates of the City of God, that heavenly city that Scripture describes in Revelation. Just past the entrance of the gates, there was a perfectly cut diamond-shaped jasper stone. I saw all the different variations of color in the stone that made up its beauty. It was perfect; flawless in color. Suddenly, we were standing on the jasper stone and Father, Son and Holy Spirit appeared as three puffs of smoke. The smoke began to swirl around us until we were hidden by it, and formed the shape of a rose bud as it wicked upward. We were surrounded by God's glory. We were in a cocoon of smoke, and we were being formed into what the Lord wanted. Only the Lord knew what would be the final result.

Steps of Understanding
(Interpretation):

This vision was about preparation. The Lord was forming a new kingdom foundation (shown by our standing on a jasper stone). He was doing a new thing in us—He had to form us afresh and anew (pictured in the three puffs of smoke forming a rose bud). The smoke was a cocoon around us, meaning what the Lord was forming was in secret. It was hidden from view until it was ready to be revealed in His timing. The key to the vision was what we were wearing once we were cocooned— wedding clothes, which represented what was being formed. When the Lord is finished with what He is forming in us, we will be preparing the bride of Christ to be a kingdom of people that loves and knows Him. This all starts with being made new. The Lord wants to form something new and fresh in us all.

Clothed in God's glory [in all its splendor and radiance]. The luster of it resembled a rare and most precious jewel, like jasper, shining clear as crystal (Rev 21:11 AMP).

*The foundation [stones] of the wall of the city were ornamented with all of the precious stones. **The first foundation [stone] was jasper,** the second sapphire, the third chalcedony (or white agate), the fourth emerald (Rev 21:19 AMP),*

Chapter 5

Adventures on the Mission Field

April, 1999: **Mexico**

We went to visit Freedom Ministries in Mexico, which was started by David Hogan.[4] At that time, his ministry had seen every form of sickness healed as well as 200 people raised from the dead.

While we were in Mexico, we stayed with David's son, Jo-D Hogan. While there, Jo-D and my husband got up at 4 AM to go to a village where they were to minister. I went back to bed because I was exhausted from the journey to Mexico. As I was sleeping, I saw a smoky white form at the foot of my bed. This form was shaking a stick at me. I realized I was propped up. Somehow, my upper body was off the bed and I was looking to my left toward the window. I saw hieroglyphics on the wall. There was a picture of a bird and a mountain; there were wiggly lines that represented water and a mask. I rebuked this scene and I went back to sleep. I was awakened again. This time, on the wall to my right, was a mask with bamboo on either side of the mask. The bamboo was bowing to the mask. I rebuked these items as well, and I went back to sleep. God was showing me that there were spirits dominating the mountains, waters, and black birds, and that the witch doctors used masks and bamboo to do their witchcraft

---

[4] *For more on David Hogan Ministries, please visit http://www.freedom-ministries.us*

deeds. He was showing me the strategy of the enemy for the mountains of Mexico.

Midmorning, the ladies came over to prepare lunch for us. Their children came with them. Because of all that had occurred hours earlier, I began to look more closely at what was happening around me. I began to pray for the women on the team, and the Lord revealed that one of the children had been developing ulcers in her stomach. As I prayed for her, she felt Jesus' power and began to tell her mother about a spirit that would sit in a tree outside her window at night. He had been tormenting her night after night for almost a year. This spirit told her that if she told her parents, he would kill them. She believed this was true because several family members died in that place because of witchcraft.

We prayed and rebuked the spirit of fear, and she was beautifully delivered. One lady had one child and wanted another, but had miscarriage after miscarriage. As I prayed for the woman, I saw a little girl (about 5 years old) sitting at her feet, being taught the Word of God. We prayed; deliverance came. Years later she told me the story of how shortly after I prayed, she passed a mass from her stomach and was able to get pregnant.

We were to go to the villages on this day. We were given instructions on how to conduct ourselves while in the villages. We were told these are tribal people. Women do not look a man in the eyes, as that would be disrespect in this culture. We were not to show our shoulders, as this would signal that we were women on the prowl for a man. One of the things that must be done if anyone was to minister at an Indian village was that all guests must eat what was set before them. Otherwise, the people would be offended because they were very poor. What they gave was the best of what they could offer us. They would eat a lesser meal, but because we were their honored guests they would kill the best animal for us. The team of missionaries needed to be able to go back to this village and establish a work without resentment based upon a visitor dishonoring the tribe.

We were warned their food was very hot. They said, on a scale of 1 -10 (10 being the hottest) their food was a 10. We were told that this may be the hottest food we'd ever tasted. Upon hearing this I prayed, *Lord, you know I can't even eat black pepper!* After this, I did not think about it anymore. When we went to the village, we ate first before the service. We all went in a line towards the table.

The tables were set with bowls full of food. We were to walk around the table until we came in front of the bowl of food that was ours. We never sat down, we stood as we ate and we ate with our hands. We were instructed how to use our tortilla as a spoon. We were to scoop the soup-like meal that was called "mole" with the tortilla. I put it up to my mouth and—incredibly--it was not hot to me. I noticed as the soup dripped down my arm it turned my skin and hand red, but it was not hot, nor did it sting as it touched my skin. It tasted like a tomato based soup that was pleasant to eat. For ten days, we ate this soup mixture with different types of animal meat in the meals. Yet, it was never hot to me. At times I would be humming while I ate, happily enjoying the meal that had been seasoned perfectly by God.

Later, Seymour mentioned that the food was extremely hot, and had messed up his digestive system. Years later, the Hogan family visited us and commented that they watched me and wondered if I was telling the truth about the food not being hot to me. They saw I had no reaction to the temperature of the food. My nose never ran, my eyes never watered. I did not have stomach problems. They concluded that it was real, that they were seeing the Father intervene for me.

The purpose for this journey was for us to be a help and strength for the Hogan team. We are all the Lord's team, and He will send us as a strengthener for others. He also gave me an extra blessing to show that He can do anything. The food being made palatable to my stomach was a personal miracle, because we all ate out of the same pot, yet the heat did not have any effect on me. I had taken this situation to the Lord, and He delivered me as He wished for me to be delivered. I did not decree it or ask for it. I just took the problem to Him in simple prayer.

I believe deliverance came because of my willingness to step into what the Lord was showing. He had brought me to war for others, not to spend all my time fighting for my own health. I had seen in a vision we were to be a reinforcement and a help to those who had been crying out to the Lord for deliverance, and He surely delivered them. The Lord wants us to look to Him and be willing. I have learned I don't always need to know the problem, I only need to do my part as a cog in the wheel of His great Kingdom plan.

2002: England

The Lord has sent us to many nations over the years. When Seymour and I travel to nations, the Lord shows us the struggles in that nation. We have seen the Lord move in many of the places we have visited. God has used us to warn pastors and ministers. God has shown us what they were up against, giving them a strategy to help them be more effective in His kingdom. This occurred when we travelled to England. As we were flying into the country, I saw a woman in the air. She was wearing a black cape with a hood. She looked like someone who worked in witchcraft. When we ministered to the people in England, we could see this spirit at work over the people. The people were in great bondage. Some had incestuous relationships. Divorces were plentiful. Witchcraft was the norm and the people were filled with superstitions. The pastor spoke of the problems they were facing in the churches. I believe Jesus gave them a strategy. After the strategy, they were bearing much fruit. People were getting inner healing from childhood wounds, and many were getting delivered.

While in England, we stayed with a couple that had opened up their home to let people from many nations come and stay. They felt the Lord had called them to host and minister to the nations. Their home was a great place for people of the Kingdom to be introduced to one another. We met people from many ministries while staying at their home, and we have sent ministers to them so they could be blessed as well.

One such minister was a pastor from Ouagadougou, Burkina Faso, Africa. When he told us where he was from, we could not believe there was such a place as Ouagadougou, Burkina Faso, Africa, but there was. It was a barren land. The country had been in a drought for years. His wife and children were there. They were down to very little supplies and they were praying for rain. When we met him he seemed very depressed and discouraged. I think he went to England for help, but did not know how he was to receive help. He seemed to have come on a wing and a prayer.

He told us about his country and how they needed supplies. Ouagadougou is on the other side of Sierra Leone. Because of the geography of his country, rain clouds hardly ever come over the mountains. When it does rain, the clouds are small and there is not much rainfall. Because of the lack of water, the crops fail and the people go hungry.

Seymour and I have seen God move many times in weather after prayer. God moved a hurricane out of the way when the weatherman said we were in the direct path of the storm, we have prayed for rain when it was needed in many situations, and have prayed for it *not* to rain and seen God answer. Consequently, we had faith that God would send rain to Ouagadougou so we prayed and encouraged the minister. It had been three years since the last rain, and eventually the wells had gone dry, but two days later, we looked at the weather report and there were clouds over Ouagadougou. By the third day, the minister called his wife. While she was talking to him on the phone, the rain was coming down so hard on her tin roof that he could hardly hear her voice. They were both crying and praising God. All the wells filled up, and the drought in Ouagadougou was over. God shows up when we pray and believe that He is the true rainmaker, and that He is Lord over all things. We just need to believe HIM! That pastor was greatly encouraged. He went back to his country blessed by the hand of the Lord. During our trip, we went to Wales, where we had an open door to visit a school that Rees Howells raised up. His students prayed fervently during WWII, and when they prayed, Hitler could not hear his spirit guides tell him what to do.

We also visited a church where the Welsh Revival, headed up by Evans Roberts, took place. As we stood outside the church in a circle to pray, I saw blue swirls swirling all over the place. The Lord said to take a picture of them; that they would show up on the camera for me. I took the pictures but it was not until I built my website, when the Lord told me to pull the pictures that I took in Wales and post them, that I actually saw them. I was amazed at how much I had captured on film. The monument to Evans Roberts had a dull surface and could not reflect light, yet a beautiful rainbow colored dove is seen in the photo. I used a digital camera so every picture would be sharp, yet a haze or white smoky swath is over Seymour and all around the church. I was amazed at what was captured.

Seymour walking in a glory haze

The shining dove appears on a dull monument

May, 2005: **Russia**

While in prayer, Seymour and I received a word from the Lord: "Go to Russia. Speak softly to the wheat: *LIVE.*" After this word came, the Lord sent in finances from everywhere. These people did not know why they were giving to us, but they heard the Lord to give. God raised up people who gave what they could to help us go. I believe that these people had a part and portion in what the Father was about to do. We then began to ask the Father where we should go in Russia. He spoke, "St. Petersburg."

We did not know anyone in Russia. In order to come to this country, you had to know someone already there. A friend of ours knew someone who was a consulate from Finland to Russia. She kindly arranged to get our letters of acceptance so that we could apply for our visa. She gave us a place to stay, and took care of all the details for our stay. The Lord led this woman completely, and before we knew it, we were on our way to St. Petersburg, Russia.

When we arrived, we had a guide who was also our driver during our stay. We found that the smog was overwhelming to the point I could not breathe. It was like being stuck in a small room with 100 non-stop smokers. My lungs began to burn, and I felt very uncomfortable, so I sought the Father. *Lord*, I said, *we will be here for ten days. The air needs to be clear so that I can breathe.* I then declared, "It needs to rain, and it needs to rain very hard."

I was not paying attention to what was happening around me. I was focused on my breathing. I suddenly noticed it was raining. Every time I said, "It needs to rain," the rain would fall in greater measure. The Finnish consulate that was in the car with us commented that she had never seen such rainfall in Russia. The rain was a tropical gale type downpour, where we could not see the roads in front of us. Our guide got anxious, and then afraid to the point that he pulled off to the side of the road to wait it out. When the rain finally cleared, we were delighted to find that the air was crystal clear. Everything felt clean and new—the Lord had washed the city for us, and it was now comfortable to breathe in. Every time the smog would build, the rain would come, and the air would become fresh again. Our driver jokingly said, "Jurena needs fresh air so the Lord has sent the rain!"

The rain came in such an abundance that the canals filled up with water. They had boats on the water that gave tours. These boats went under bridges that were a football field apart from the other. The city had never seen this before. So they did not think to stop the boat tours lest the water caused the boats to get lodged under the bridges. We were going under bridges where the tops of the seats were scraping underneath, and we had to lie down in the seats in order to get through! Seymour, who has an engineering background, showed the conductor how to shimmy the boat through so we wouldn't get stuck. We were amazed at what the Lord had done.

The woman who had gotten us into Russia took us to a church that was started by an American who had a Russian wife. This church had great influence in Russia. He had a radio program that went over a large section of the old Soviet

Union. The Lord opened the door for us to pray and prophesy over this nation. The Lord also opened the door for Seymour to speak to the people and for me to lead worship on the following Wednesday service. Seymour kept using words and phrases like, "The glory of God, God's glory moving through the whole earth, etc." This seed went into the pastor, and several years later we were excited to learn that he held an event called "The Glory Conference." Hallelujah, the Father knows how to plant seeds.

That night, there were pastors from all over the old Soviet bloc, and they wanted me to bless the church, as an American, with worship. They arranged for me a few instrumentalists to play along as I sang. I had a woman who played piano, and another woman who played cello. The quality of their playing was on an orchestra level. They told me they had made professional Christian CDs, but they longed for the anointing over their music. They did not yet experience this touch from God. That night as I began to sing, the presence of the Lord filled the room, and the pastor of the church raised his hands in abandoned worship before the Lord. The pastors from the other churches saw their leader raising his hands in worship, and they commented, "Pastor has gone into Pentecost!" Earlier, we heard some of the pastors speak against anything that had a move of God upon it, as if they were afraid of God.

One of the pastors that came into St. Petersburg was a pastor from Vyborg, Russia. This was a coastal town on the Baltic Sea facing Finland. He invited us to come to his church and help him for a few days while we were there. We took a train, and after a few hours we arrived in this small coastal town. He told us that he and his wife were extremely discouraged. He had told the Lord when he arrived at the service in St. Petersburg that if they did not see real Christianity, they were going to give up all ministry and quit, because they did not see the point in continuing. When they heard Seymour speak, and me singing, and saw their leader respond to the worship, their heart became hopeful, so they asked us to please come.

Yet they, too, were very afraid of the Spirit of God. The pastor often would say he did not believe in any manifestations of The Spirit. We did not try to correct him. We simply loved on him and served wherever he wanted us to. He asked us to speak at his church. Seymour gave the message and asked if anyone wanted prayer. The pastor had told us earlier not to lay hands on anyone, because he was afraid of what would happen. So Seymour and I did not touch a soul, we just bowed our heads, and people began to fall out under the power of God. We were amazed and grateful at what the Lord did.

During our time visiting with the pastor, he told us that he and another man would go out and street witness to the people in a nearby park in order to help bring a few souls to Christ. He said he had not seen any souls give their heart to God, which made him very discouraged. He invited us to go with him.

The first woman we came upon had been bleeding for months. She was very thin, and sickly. She and her children lived as a gypsy family. We asked if we could pray for her via translation. We prayed for her, and the Lord beautifully healed her, drying up the issue of blood within an hour as she followed us around. She began to come to church. We prayed for many people that day, and gave many of them prophetic words and encouragement.

One such man felt God's presence so strong he drew back and did not want us to touch him. They seemed very superstitious, but the Lord touched him just the same. We left this pastor with an iPod that had music from a spirit-filled minister whose music was full of Lord Holy Spirit's power. I was once sick and listened to the sound of it, and was completely healed. They listened and commented that they loved it. We knew this music was filled with what they were at first afraid of: The Spirit of God. This was the wheat the Lord was telling us to speak to, to declare it should live. This church and its pastor were about to die and abandon the work they had been called to. They wrote us many times to tell us how blessed they were, and what God was doing in Vyborg. The Father loved these dear ones and knew their hearts. He sent us to strengthen the feeble hands with no condemnation, but instead showed them the way toward His will for them. They walked in everything we instructed them to do, and they gave God the glory for what He had done.

July, 2006: **Venezuela**

We were invited to go to Bolívar, Venezuela with a group of Spanish pastors. It was a move to unify the pastors in Venezuela. While there, television crews interviewed us. We also had an opportunity to speak on the national radio network and proclaim a prophetic word outward from the city to the nation. Seymour was asked to speak at one of the largest churches in the area. The pastor heard us speak of the things the Lord was doing. He was hungry for God and had never seen the presence of God move, but the presence of God was tangible as we sat and talked of what Jesus was doing throughout His church.

He asked us to pray for him and his family. He was a Word of Faith minister and believed that only Word of Faith prayers should be spoken. I prayed that the Lord would provide for him in a supernatural way. He did not believe in lack or being in need, so he was truly puzzled that I would speak such a word over him. After all, they had a large church and all was good. I knew that he thought I was missing it. Even so, as I then prayed over Venezuela, I saw a man in a vision. He had on a military outfit and was carrying a gun. It was as if he were holding a gun on someone and making demands. I told the pastors what I saw. They said nothing but knew what was happening in the political realm. They were feeling the rumblings of change, and knew I was speaking the truth.

As we were departing the country, we were leaving with a group of missionaries from the mountains of Venezuela. They told us they were closing down missions in the mountains because the nation was sending all the missionaries out of the country. We had made it in just under the radar.

Years later, I looked Venezuela up on the Internet. Wikipedia reported, "On August 15, 2007, Chávez proposed a broad package of measures as part of a constitutional reform. Among other measures, he called for an end to presidential term limits and proposed limiting central bank autonomy, strengthening state expropriation powers, and providing for public control over international reserves as part of an overhaul of Venezuela's constitution. In accordance with the 1999 constitution, Chávez proposed the changes to the constitution, which were then approved by the National Assembly. The final test was a December 2, 2007 referendum. The referendum was defeated, with 51% of the voters rejecting the amendments proposed by Chávez.[46] On 15 February 2009, Chávez won a referendum to eliminate term limits." Political change had come to Venezuela, just as the Lord had revealed to me.

June, 2007: **Israel**

Israel reached out to the Church, and we were among those who had an opportunity to be present at the Knesset. At this time, Seymour read the love letter to Israel he had written years before. As the love letter was being read, I remembered the vision of the two olive trees that had come together as one and how beautiful it was. This was a divine moment in time. The Lord loves to take us into battle so that His eternal purposes and rewards are made manifest in and through us.

Chapter 6

The Golden Path

April 17, 2008

If we are saved, we are seated in heavenly places in Christ Jesus.

> *Even when we were dead in sins, hath quickened us together with Christ, (by grace ye are saved) And hath raised us up together, and made us sit together in heavenly places in Christ Jesus (Eph 2:5-6):*

In a vision, I saw myself on a golden path. I felt an overwhelming sense of love flowing all around me, and somehow realized that Heaven was wanting to give me all things. I felt unworthy, but they were rejoicing that I was willing to receive. (Fear not, little flock, it is the Father's good pleasure to give you the kingdom, *Luke 12:32*.) The path was moving like a conveyor belt, and I was given various gifts as I moved along the path.

The first gift was a set of keys. These keys represented salvation, repentance, forgiveness, walking by faith, hearing God, obedience, purity, and holiness. There were other related keys, as well. (These are all keys that followers of Christ must use in their daily walk. They are the basics of Christianity.) Then I passed a river, and somehow knew that it was the River of Life. I stepped off the path and went into the river ankle-deep. Jesus was there holding my hand. I said, "Lord, I want to go deeper." He took me deeper, and the water came up to my knees.

Then we went even deeper and before I knew it, the water was over my head. I realized I could breathe beneath the water. Jesus was there with me the whole time, training me how to go deeper with Him. The river represented flowing with the Spirit. It was over my head because I was learning how to rest in Him and not be in control, thereby letting the life of God flow through me and out of me, letting God's way be the controlling factor in my life. *"Trust in the Lord with all your heart and lean not on your own understanding (Prov 3:5 NIV)."*

Once a river takes over, *you* are controlled by *it*. You cannot direct the flow. This is what it is like following God—He wants to direct the flow of the spirit in your life. We take the keys with us on our journey, and the river will take us where we need to use them. Both the keys and the river are part of the Golden Path, the place we always navigate back to, as we journey.

Next, I saw a waterfall that was like oil. This scene was in a beautiful, tropical garden with lush, green foliage. In the distance, a golden waterfall of oil rained down into a beautiful pool. The waterfall represented the anointing that God gives us to do His will. I knew to go and wash myself in the oil.

Afterwards, I was back on the golden path, where I came upon a huge flat-screen television. It was larger and taller than I was, and it filled my whole vision. My feet seemed to be stuck in the golden path in front of this television. I could not move forward. As I watched, I was dismayed to see it was playing negative reruns of my past. The reruns were of times when I had failed, or when people had failed me. I knew what the Lord was saying to me. He had given me the keys to the Kingdom, and I needed to train myself to walk in the freedom of each key.

> *I will give you the keys of the kingdom of Heaven; and whatever you bind on earth shall have been bound in Heaven, and whatever you loose on earth shall have been loosed in Heaven (Matt 16:19 NASB).*

Through Jesus, I was washed, anointed, and seated in heavenly places, but I was stuck reliving the negative incidents of my past instead of seeing His future for me (my original design from the beginning of time). My past had my attention, not the wonderful plans He had for me. Isn't that what we so often do? Jesus gives us keys to bring us through our circumstances into deliverance. He brings revival and refreshes us. He uses us and anoints us. But the moment the enemy reminds us of our past or of things that have hurt us, we are stuck looking at the reruns in our minds. We are like a "deer in the headlights," unable to move forward because we keep replaying what is behind. We are stuck in the past on the way to our future.

This vision is key to all saints, and something most of us do not quite fathom. Our spirit man is saved and has the ability to walk with God and move with God. But it is the soul man that we

Kingdom Keys

I have found the way to get moving forward is through repentance and forgiveness. They are two of the most powerful keys of the Kingdom.

have problems with (as pictured by the TV in the above vision). We forget that our souls have been discipled by hell. That is why the Lord said, "Go and make disciples" *(Matt 28:19)*. We must learn how to walk in the Spirit, and let our Spirit man lead, *not* the soul (which has its roots in the darkness we have come from).

This is why we must be transformed. We have seen so many people that wanted to work for God. But as soon as they step out and go so far (especially if they are effective), something in the soul or their past comes up and they are stopped in their tracks from going any further. The work of the Lord is once again stopped and hindered. The spirit is willing, but the flesh or soul is weak in doing the will of God *(Mark 14:38, Psalms 73:26)*. So many have not allowed the Lord to develop their spirit man, and they remain spiritual infants. The Lord wants us to become mature, capable, spiritual people. Everything He speaks is in and from the Spirit. He said, "The words that I have spoken to you are *spirit*..."

It is the Spirit Who gives life [He is the Life-giver]; the flesh conveys no benefit whatever [there is no profit in it]. The words (truths) that I have been speaking to you are spirit and life (John 6:63 AMP).

The flesh or soul sees no profit in it, so our spirit man must step into the things of God. We must crucify the soul and its passions with the life of Christ living through us; we do this by living a repented life.

I acknowledged my sin to You, and my iniquity I did not hide. I said, I will confess my transgressions to the Lord [continually unfolding the past till all is told] — then You [instantly] forgave me the guilt and iniquity of my sin. Selah [pause, and calmly think of that] (Psalms 32:5 AMP).

Too many in the Church live in the guilt of our souls vs. the freedom that lives and resides in our spirit. This is not about being right in our salvation. It is a knowing, an assurance that we can stand in the presence of the King because our hearts are clean.

In 1998, we were living in Cherry Hill, NJ. This was during a particularly difficult time in my life, and the Lord was trying to get me to forgive and give up some things that were keeping me separated from Him. But I did not understand what he was saying. I shook my fist at Him angrily, asking, "What are you doing to me?" He gently replied: "My grace is sufficient for you." With these words, I saw a picture of the cross. I was standing before the cross, and it became a sieve, like you would use to sift flour. I walked through the mesh-like sieve and the stuff that I was battling stayed on the front side of the cross. I was on the other side rejoicing. I was free of all that had been weighing me down! It was glorious; I felt light as a feather. Repentance changed everything. Even my personality and attitude changed. I thought that when people said I needed to repent they were telling me I was worthless, that I had no value. I thought the person was being self-righteous and judging me. I was so wrong. I finally began to realize that repentance was the only door to freedom and power.

God showed me the beauty of repentance. It was His way of removing the enemy out of my life, which allowed me to get free from the torment. The freedom was overwhelming. In my immaturity, I went on a "witch-hunt," looking for things from which to repent. I later learned that God leads us to our different "television moments" so that we can get greater and greater freedom in Him. Repentance became a wonderful experience for me. It is in God's plan for us all. Everything He gives brings life.

During this time I learned about repentance and how important it is. That it was important to defeating my enemies and moving into maturity. The Lord was showing me this truth. He said, "The enemy says about us: 'I do not care if you are saved, I know the investment I have put in you from the time you were born *(Psalm 51:5)*. At a time of weakness, I can pull that chain—whatever you don't give to Jesus, *I own it.*'"

I have learned to take everything to the cross. The more weakness I give to the Lord, the more protection I receive against the evil one *(John 5:18)*. Many parts of our souls need to be born of God again and again. I have learned to use my "God tool"—repentance. I have found this tool to be powerful in that it pulls down every thought in me that exalts itself against the will of God for me.

> We use our powerful **God-tools for smashing warped philosophies, tearing down barriers erected against the truth of God,** *fitting every loose thought and emotion and impulse into the structure of life shaped by Christ. Our tools are ready at hand for clearing the ground of every obstruction and building lives of obedience into maturity (2 Cor 10:5-6, The Message).*

The Lord began to show me how to be victorious in Him by revealing the enemy's structure over this world. He taught me there are four negative levels in our souls that must be overcome.   What I saw was a military structure: the first level consisted of the negative privates that govern our soul. We see their manifestation in the family structure. Family attitudes and generational curses are part of this first battle (the privates).

The next level was where all the wounds that are inflicted to keep us relationally broken off and separated were in operation. These were the sergeants, and their job was to keep us divided one from another. The sergeants work to form people groups. Although we need relationships because the Father has made us this way, the sergeants use this for the enemy's purposes. So now we are partitioned into groups on likes and dislikes and attitudes. We do this all the time, as naturally as breathing. We call these groups by ethnic names or by describing a generation, like Baby Boomers, Generation X, Millennials, etc.. Each of these groups has a single mindset that the sergeants control through generational deception and wounding.

The next level is the lieutenants. These leaders control regions of people groups (grabbing these from the sergeants to increase their own numbers as much as possible). You can sense their control when you come into the cities. Most people will have an attitude that reflects the city they live in. This is an acquired attitude, which we add to the familiar spirits from our family structure, growing up.

For example, New Yorkers will have an attitude of abruptness, while the different counties or regions of New York will produce people whose language and attitudes will be different from other areas. If you travel to the South, people will be more laid back, while the northern cities are fast paced. Generally speaking, those from the "heartland," or Midwest, hold traditional values while the coastal cities are more open to extreme ways of living. Others are stuck in structures of bondage to one another's opinions for acceptance and affirmation, not wanting to swim against the currents of mainstream thought. These are the basic social structures.

The generals, or world rulers, are the leadership forces that are established over entire countries. Most Americans are identified as Americans when we enter a country. We have an attitude of freedom that couples itself to the idea that we can demand what we want. Other countries will have atmospheres of depression or oppression. These generals can control multiple people groups at a time. We saw this during the rise of Hitler and many oppressed regimes, and we are still seeing it today. All these spirits keep us in a state of broken relationships.

The Lord has given us powerful heavenly counterparts to defeat the enemy's structures:

> *For He rescued us from the domain of darkness, and transferred us to the kingdom of His beloved Son, in whom we have redemption, the forgiveness of sins. He is the image of the invisible God, the firstborn of all creation. For by Him all things were created, both in the heavens and on earth, visible and invisible, whether thrones or*

dominions or rulers or authorities—all things have been created through Him and for Him (Col 1:13-16).

Against the rulers (privates), the Lord has given us authorities. These are our personal angels (guardian angels) that work in our lives on a personal level *(Matt 18:10)*. Against the powers (sergeants) the Lord has given us His rulers, angels who help people groups *(Exo 15:16)*. Against world forces of darkness (lieutenants) the Lord has given us dominion *(Dan 10:13)*. Against the spiritual forces of wickedness (generals), the Lord has given us His throne, where all decisions are made *(1 Kings 20:10)*.

We can see from this structure it is kingdom against kingdom, with *us* being the prize. Therefore, we must yield to the foundational plan, which is the cross. The cross removes what the enemy has planted in our hearts from our youth. Each comes to collect what they own. Jesus must be the full owner of the soulish part of our human nature. He told us how to overcome in John 14:30-31:

I will not speak much more with you, for the ruler of the world is coming, and he has nothing in Me; but so that the world may know that I love the Father, I do exactly as the Father commanded Me. Get up, let us go from here.

The evidence of the Lord's ground in us is the fruit of the Spirit. Signs that the enemy still has ground in our hearts are hurt, fear, lust, anger, guilt, shame etc.. Sin is what these forces use to derail lives. The more of God we have, and more obedience we walk in, the more victory comes into our lives. The more we yield to the enemy and do not let the Lord redeem and cleanse the heart, the more calamity we will see around us. Draw nigh to God, and He will draw nigh to you *(James 4:8)*.

So Jesus gave us beautiful gifts called *forgiveness* and *repentance* that heal what the privates have done to us, helping us come out of our people group, and therefore, changing our generations. The Lord is still speaking to us as He did Cain: *"Cain, sin is knocking at your door, but you must master it."* We must still master these things in order to effectively defeat satan's attacks.

We recognize, and will not become part of, what is going on in the region we are living in because we are coming in the opposite spirit *(2 Cor 10:14)*. We take our countries through the change of our nature and our hearts; we escape the mindsets with its traps and emotional ruts that our particular people group falls into as we discern other people groups overtaken in a fault. To take that world ruler, the King's throne must rule through His people, leading them to begin taking ground *(Eph 6:12)*.

We are the salt of the world *(Matt 5:13)*. We do this by first taking our own heart ground that gives us power to move up the spiritual change. If we will walk in the light as He is in the light, we can have unbroken fellowship one with another *(John 1:7)*. But if we [really] are living and walking in the light, as He [Himself] is in the light, we have [true, unbroken] fellowship with one another, and the blood of Jesus Christ His Son cleanses (removes) us from all sin and guilt [keeps us cleansed from sin in all its forms and manifestations].

When the light of Jesus is truly manifested in all areas of our life, we will cause others to come out of the darkness they are living in. If they are seeking Him, they will see His change in us, and look to the Lord themselves. Everything the Lord has given us will be manifested. The keys to the Kingdom, the anointing that is upon us, will be seen by all. We will continually wash ourselves in that River of Life that the Lord has provided. It all starts with dealing with the "privates" that have had their foot on our necks through the hurts, wounds, and generational injustices. We do this through the act of turning and dealing with our own hearts before the Lord, repenting and forgiving all the way. This is the pathway of the cross!

Kingdom Keys

Too many in the Church live in the guilt of our souls vs. the freedom that lives and resides in our spirit.

Chapter 7

Angelic Helpers Sent by the Father

One night at Harp and Bowl (our weekly time of seeking the Lord in prayer and worship based on the biblical model of 24/7 worship going up before the Lord), the Lord showed me that He was sending His helpers. My spirit was opened up and I was able to see into the heavenlies. I began to see the helpers coming down a ladder from Heaven to Earth.

> *He came and took the scroll from the right hand of him who sat on the throne. And when he had taken it, the four living creatures and the twenty-four elders fell down before the Lamb. Each one had a harp and they were holding golden bowls full of incense, which are the prayers of the saints (Rev 5:7-8 NIV).*

> *But of which of the angels hath he said at any time, Sit thou on my right hand, Till I make thine enemies the footstool of thy feet? Are they not all ministering spirits, sent forth to do service for the sake of them that shall inherit salvation (Heb 1:13-14)?*

April 18, 2008

On October 7, 2007, the Lord shared that He would be sending us helpers. At the time, I did not know what He meant, so I pondered this word in my heart. In April, the Lord told me that He would be introducing me to my angelic helpers.[5]

Sally: Causing Things to Bloom

The first helper's name was Sally, who was touching flowers that had not yet bloomed. She was wearing a lovely dress that looked like a pinafore, or jumper. She walked up to me and said simply, "Hello, my name is Sally; I cause things to grow." Later, I found out that the name, Sally, means to cause to bloom. She reached out and touched my heart, and a large flower came out of my chest.

I then looked up, and saw a field as far as the eye could see from left to right. The field was full of flower buds and stalks. These stalks stood about 6′ tall with blooms that had not yet opened. She said to me, "These are all the seeds you have planted that have not yet bloomed." I knew they were all the things that Seymour and I had done for the Lord over the years—giving, helping, and sacrificing for the Kingdom of God. *Give and it will be given to you. A good measure, pressed down, shaken together and running over (Luke 6:38 NIV).* Yet, we knew we had not quite seen the blessing over our lives for what we had sown.

Sally began to run down the middle of the field, her arms stretched out horizontally and pointing to the right and to the left. As she ran, every flower she passed bloomed on her right and on her left. She cried out, "Run with me!" I began to run with her. Flowers were blooming all over my body. She said, "Run! Don't let the blessings overtake you!" With this statement, a picture came into my mind of what we do when we finally receive the things for which we have been praying and seeking—things like ministry growth and all sorts of blessings. At first, we suffer and go through all manner of hardship, being in a lowly state, walking humbly before the Lord. But once we receive the blessings, we're no

---

[5] *Regarding my experiences with angels, I must continually stress that I do not want anyone to take away the idea that you could order your own "Pogo" or "Fetch," or any other angel you read about here. Please note that it was the Lord Who initiated the angelic activity, and understand that these are ministering angels who respond to HIS purposes and plans.*

longer hungry, so our priorities change. As the blessings overtake us, we can become prideful and arrogant.

While David was running from Saul, he was an honorable man. He had a chance to get revenge by killing Saul in the cave; but because of his integrity, he would not touch God's anointed. After Saul died and David became king, he changed. He killed the husband of Bathsheba while plotting to have her for himself, and to cover up their adultery. The blessings of becoming king of Israel overtook David.

This is what Sally meant when she said, "Don't let the blessings overtake you." She was telling me to run hard for the Lord, to keep going as I did at the first when I was hungry, forsaken, abandoned, and persecuted. As I ran, I could not keep up with her. She saw I needed help, so she reached down and put wings on my ankles, and I was then able to run without too much effort. No matter how strong we are in the Lord, Scripture reminds us of our weakness: *For they loved the praise of men more than the praise of God (John 12:43 KJV)*.

The Lord sent this angel after much dialoguing with Him concerning the situation that we were not blessed after so many years of giving to people and ministries. I had often heard it preached that if you gave, then God would give back to you. It happened sometimes, but more often it did not occur in my life. I began to think something was wrong with me, and that somehow the Lord was angry. After prayer, I met Sally who showed me that nothing was left unnoticed or was lost by the Lord. He kept everything that we had sowed for His appointed time *(Prov 16:16)*. The blessings He was releasing to us were not only financial but eternal blessings, which is so much greater than the temporal things of the here and now *(Psalm 21:5-6)*.

I had learned that a lot of what is taught in the Church has brought confusion about the ways of God. This vision gave me balance and peace that He had not forgotten my giving or my sacrifice. It was up to Him how my reward came, and not up to me or my expectations of the reward (which—if left unchecked by Him—would bring bitterness toward God and confusion in my heart). I was grateful that He would choose how to bless my giving. He does all things perfectly in its season. It is His strength that keeps us from going our own way and doing our own thing.

The Lord sent this angel to me several times after this visitation. We would run the fields together to make sure I understood that I needed to run, and not let the blessings overtake me. One such time I outran Sally, and she smiled as she said, "Well done." The Lord was training me not to fall for any traps.

Specifinon: Bringing a New Day, a New Way

This next angel's name was spoken to me first, but I was unable to receive it, because of doubt, unbelief, and the religious spirit I was entertaining. Finally in November of 2012, I was able to hear this name. It was the day before Thanksgiving, and the Lord spoke to me to thank Him for the helper and the ministering spirit He had given us. The Lord took me back to that moment when He was giving me the names of the angels He was sending to help, and I had heard the name Specifinon. At the time, the name just seemed too unusual, so I stumbled over my own preconceived ideas of what the angels would or should be like.

This time, I saw Specifinon standing on a hill overlooking the horizon, and he opened up the way before us. He brought a new day, a new way. We saw the manifestation of this angel in our lives many times. As you read further, you will see the Lord sent us to many cities and regions. We were sent to do specific things to open up new things in those regions, and this angel was part of those works.

We needed Specifinon desperately. At the time, we were going through a rough stretch where many ungodly words were being spoken that were both harmful and hurtful. Because of the ministrations and refreshing this angel brought, I was able to pray for those who spoke all manner of evil against us, and do it from a pure heart. The Father's words are true. Life came to me, and I was able to run with the Lord and move on to the next assignments He had for us unhindered by bitterness or hurt. This was an awesome time of spiritual growth and character building.

Pogo: Carrying the Saints Over Troubled Waters

Next, I saw Pogo, but, again, I refused to believe the name he was giving me. It was too hard for me to receive such a strange name, so I began to rebuke him. But he did not move, no matter how much I rebuked and pleaded the blood of

Jesus. Finally, I realized I was resisting the Lord, and that the angel had been sent to me by Him, so I accepted him and his ministry. Pogo was walking on tall stilts. He said he carried people through troubled waters. I saw myself being carried over water that was teeming with alligators (the alligators represented lies from people having great influence over others).

I realized Pogo had a necessary place in our lives. It seemed that while Specifinon's ministry opened the way into new things, I believe this angel was sent by the Lord to carry us through very troubling times, when lies are all around us, to get us to those new things. The enemy and his demons are all filled with accusation, and it's this accusing spirit that causes lies to surround God's people. The journey is made a bit easier when we learn how to receive the help our Father sends to us.

Whirlwind: Mover of Things for Kingdom Purposes

Whirlwind was another angel necessary to what the Father was doing in our lives. His job was to move things—to carry things in and to bring things out. We saw the work of this angel many times in our lives. We would want to meet different people that, at the time, we thought were important to what the Lord was doing and what we were seeing in the Spirit. But then the Lord moved these people away from us, or we would have a meeting set up with a popular church magazine and we would hear the Lord speak, "Not now; do not go that way." We also saw the Lord put us in strategic places where others would marvel at how He had placed us there. People would say that they have been at jobs and places for years and they had not received the favor that they saw over our lives. The things that happened were supernatural.

Angel Fisher: Deliverer and Freedom Giver

Help from the next angel, Angel Fisher, has been marvelous to behold. This angel is a deliverer and a freedom giver.

In the church the Lord has given us to steward, we encourage the prophetic gifts. I had redesigned a staff that the Lord had given me through a brother who created walking sticks. He had given Seymour and me each one of our choosing. In our church worship, we wave banners as part of our expression of love to the Father (SoS 6:10, 6:4). One day, banners were taken from the pulpit and placed down the aisles of the church during our time of worship. The Lord spoke to me to take my staff and strike each banner and keep going until I went to the threshold of the front exit doors.

After about 15 minutes, a woman was driving past our church, and felt compelled to make a u-turn and come back so she could come into the building. She came in crying and shaking as she asked, "What must I do to be saved?" I led her to the Lord, and she immediately gave us all of her drugs. She was the local drug dealer in a trailer park near the church, and the Lord had decided it was her day to begin a new life of freedom.

We are still seeing the Lord bring souls to us. Many of these people are in all types of places of drug addictions, and we are rejoicing that the Lord is delivering them and setting them free. The amazing thing is they are getting saved during praise and worship. We realized what we were seeing: "The fish are jumping into the boat!" Truly, the Lord is saving and keeping those that have no hope, and He is giving them a way out.

This same woman decided, after one year of salvation, that she would go back to her heroin addiction, which she had not done for 2-3 yrs. She testified to us that she and one of her friends were shooting up. She said the young lady watched her as she took needle after needle and could not get high or get the taste in her mouth. Her panicked friend told her, "You are going to overdose and die!" After five failed attempts to get high, she broke down and began to repent in front of her friend, finally acknowledging that drugs were no longer a part of her life. The friend, looking on, knew she was seeing a miracle, and gave her heart to the Lord. Angel Fisher had delivered completely.

From this one incident, a new wave of souls came to the Lord. They, too, were weak and tried to do drugs again, and the drugs did not work. The Lord has been delivering the souls He is bringing in, we are just spectators to what the Lord is doing in His house. All we can do is praise Him for the testimonies of His work. Our job during all this was simply to love them and accept them and teach them to talk to God for themselves. We continue to marvel at what the Lord is saying to these young converts. Later in my story you will hear how Jesus told me the way He will take care of His souls and raise them up.

Hopper: Skipping the Unnecessary Things

The next angel was Hopper, who helped us "hop" over what was not necessary. So many times we do things that are not really the Lord's will. I believe Hopper helped us hop over unnecessary things and bypass them to learn something new. Without this angel, we would have spent more time doing "good ideas" instead of "God ideas." With a limited amount of time given to us in this world, it is important to focus only on what the Father has for us to do.

Other angels were also sent to us, when we needed what they had for us in various seasons and situations:

Faith, Rank, and Striper

> Faith had a shield that went over our own faith. I believe he protects and covers our faith.

> Rank was actually two angels that were standing side-by-side and shoulder-to-shoulder. Their job was to keep order. They kept everything organized so they could maintain order in the rank and file.

> Striper's job was to heal specific illnesses and oversee specific healings (*...with His stripes we are healed; Isaiah 53:5*).

The testimonies of healings have been amazing. One woman was in a hospital dying of AIDS. Her daughter was an unbeliever, but she did not want her mother to die so she called us in to pray. Her mother was in a coma and had gangrene in one of her legs. She was not expected to live. But the Lord showed her mercy, and raised her up off of her sick bed to the amazement of her doctors. Then, the doctors said she would never walk again. Within one week, her leg was healed and she was walking her grandson around in the local Walmart.

Her daughter and son-in-law were headed for divorce. They came to us for help since they saw the Lord move in the life of their mother so powerfully. They gave their hearts to the Lord, and He saved their marriage. Now, they are being wonderfully used by God. They have won many to the Lord, and are raising up people in their age group to be firebrands for God. Many people have met them and stated that they can't believe that they are so young in the Lord. They appear to be seasoned saints of God. It is the Lord Who is doing the work—He sets His people on fire when they have a personal encounter with Him *(1 John 3:2)*!

Freedom, Fetch, and Drench

> ➢ Freedom helps with setting the captives free.
> ➢ Fetch brings the "new" from Heaven.
> ➢ Drench brings the outpouring.

We have seen Fetch bring many new things to us from the Father's hand. It has changed our way of thinking about the Kingdom of God. I must say that we have seen all these manifestations in our walk with the Father. We are an army with the Lord, and He has sent these angels to support and assist in carrying out kingdom purposes. Surely Elisha saw this host of angels going about their job assignments from the Father. Elisha's eye saw the glory and the kingdom at work for him and his servant. We need to have faith that God will do it again and again for His servants.

> *Now when the attendant of the man of God had risen early and gone out, behold, an army with horses and chariots was circling the city. And his servant said to him, "Alas, my master! What shall we do?" So he answered, "Do not fear, for those who are with us are more than those who are with them." Then Elisha prayed and said, "O Lord, I pray, open his eyes that he may see." And the Lord opened the servant's eyes and he saw; and behold, the mountain was full of horses and chariots of fire all around Elisha. When they came down to him, Elisha prayed to the Lord and said, "Strike this people with blindness, I pray." So He struck them with blindness according to the word of Elisha (2 Kings 6:15-18).*

Once, as I sat resting, I saw an angel standing right in front of me, at the right side of the throne. He was dressed in white, and had a golden sash that went over his right shoulder and came together and rested on his left hip. The distinguishing feature about him was his hair, because it was yellow. It was an unnatural color, almost like crayon yellow. I said nothing to him, and he said nothing to me. Since angels in other visions told me their names and their functions, I flippantly asked, "So, what is your name?" Because I was full of doubt, I was a bit sarcastic. I thought I was imagining these things.

He stood there and did not say a word. After a while, I asked again, "What is your name?" He responded, "Raphael." He said, "I dispense glory and truth." When he said that, faith suddenly rose up in my spirit. I asked, "Will you give it to me?" He said, "Yes, and much more."

This experience was very interesting to me, because I had never heard of an angel by the name of Raphael. I only knew of Michael and Gabriel as mentioned in the Bible. In order to know if I was really seeing an angel, I looked on the Internet under "names of angels." I found that an angel named Raphael had appeared to many people throughout history, and was known as the healing angel. Also, Judaism recognizes Raphael as one of the four angels of the Presence: Michael, Gabriel, Raphael, and Uriel. I thought it was interesting that Raphael said he dispenses glory and truth. Another thing I noted was that most of the angels I saw or interacted with did not have wings, but had a banner draped across their chest. I believe the banners signified dominion.

*And in the middle of the lampstands I saw one like a son of man, clothed in a robe reaching to the feet, and girded across His chest with a **golden sash** (Rev 1:13).*

Chapter 8

Hungering for More of Him

April 18, 2003

While attending a revival, I saw two 20-foot high angels wearing white robes. They were as tall as the ceiling of the church we were attending, and each had a candle in his left hand. The angel on the right had a bowl that overflowed with golden oil, and the oil dripped to the floor. The angel on the left had a sword in his hand. The sharp edge of the sword was pointed to the floor.

The angel on the right addressed me and said, "The rest is coming; great things will be done in the spirit of rest. I will send Rest. The Angel called Rest is coming, and Comfort is with him. Many things will be done through Rest. The oil is flowing here. My name is Anointing; Power is on the other side. There will be many miracles that take place in this church. Watch how they take place. Get acquainted with these signs, for they will follow you; Anointing, Rest, Power, and Comfort will follow you. See, the flow is easy. We do the Father's bidding. If you learn to watch us, you will do many things. We do the work—what is needed is in the oil that flows from the cups in our hands. Just stay in the flow. See, the healing strength is in the flow. The anointing is living."

These two angels were Anointing and Power. Anointing brings the work and Power executes the work. The anointing angel said, "Father sends us as gifts when there is hunger and open hearts." I asked, "Will you give it to me?" He replied, "That which you are seeing is the impartation. It is yours and Seymour's tonight. Father has seen the hunger, and you shall be filled."

There was a girl next to me. She was crying out with all her heart, "Father, Father, I hunger for you!" He said, "See, see the hunger. That is why we are here. Wash in the oil, and Power will touch the oil and make it one. Power and Anointing are one."

It's amazing when the Spirit of God talks to you. One word can be said, but with that word God gives revelation to what is heard. The angel named Power never spoke to me. I knew why he would not speak. I instantly had the understanding that the angels speak to us according to what we have walked in and what our lives demonstrate. I had an anointing in worship and in the Word, but I did not yet walk in the power of God. Not on the level that this angel was giving. I realized that if I wanted what he could impart, I needed to have a cup that he could fill. I did not, as of yet, possess that cup, but because I saw him; I knew one day I would walk in the power this angel carried. I knew in order to walk where miracles are seen constantly; I had to have an anointing with power. These gifts operate as one unit on this level.

Kingdom Keys

The angel named Power never spoke to me. I knew why he would not speak. I instantly had the understanding that the angels speak to us according to what we have walked in and what our lives demonstrate. Although I had an anointing in worship and in the Word, I did not yet walk in the power of God. Not on the level that this angel was giving. I realized that if I wanted what he could impart, I needed to have a cup that he could fill.

I understood that our lives have a sound. We can sound like thankfulness, worship, praise, love—or we can sound like depression, anger, bitterness, and filthiness of soul. We all hear these sounds consciously or unconsciously.

Heaven clearly hears what sound our lives make. I knew they were looking for the part of Jesus I possessed in my heart—not to judge me, but to find a common ground of communication. So I asked, "What holy sound does our heart make that can be spoken to by the Spirit of God?

Yet You are holy, O You who are enthroned upon the praises of Israel *(Psalms 22:3 NASB).*

One of the ways God the Father allows us tremendous wrestlings of spiritual warfare is when we give to Him what is truly due Him—complete honorable praise to the audience of ONE. This is when praise and worship shifts from the crowd to the Lord God alone. When this occurs, God the Father parks His throne over such praise, and world rulers over cities must yield and give up their former airwaves. This is when God the Father possesses all things as KING. Sending His Kingdom down to those who will truly walk in the faith of the ages. This is a precursor to the moves of God and sustainer of when commands go forth from the Throne Room – from Heaven to Earth, carrying out His will. This is the highest form of praise and worship we can offer the Lord God Almighty, with Jesus our Christ seated beside Him from Earth. This is when the Lord God possesses His praise.

The Lord inhabits the praises of His people. Another way to say it is: the Lord *possesses* the praises of His people. God owns our perfect praise, and in that perfect praise the prophetic is revealed. If you want to hear from God, begin to love on Him with praise and worship—not to praise Him in the sound of the music or the beautiful voice or the best performance—but to praise Him with heartfelt love songs. This opens the very heavens as you "enter His gates with praise and His courts with thanksgiving," and you can begin to hear God. Heaven is drawn to perfect praise and, from that perfect place, Heaven can speak to us.

But, sadly, too many times church worship is a dead form or an entertainment avenue for people to further their own fame. It can even be a snare to those who are not mindful of the enemy's devices. Many worship leaders have fallen into sexual sin, as their anointing is one easily accessed by satan, since he was the first worship leader and understands the many vulnerable aspects and temptations connected to worship. (Praise and worship are, among other things, an intimate communication between the Creator and the created—the created responding with all its being to the One Who started the conversation with us. But satan, the imposter, tries to come in and divert our attention to anywhere but our Father God where it belongs—even to ourselves).

Many people have "their" songs, songs that move their soul. The song is usually about them and their need to be loved by God. This is fine as a start—these songs should bring us into the presence of the Lord and make us thankful to Him. But sadly, many are stuck at this place. Instead of it drawing them deeper into an intimate place of communion with the Lord, where they are consumed by His very presence, their "worship" becomes all about them and their need.

At some point, this becomes the worship of self. The focus is not on the Lord, the Creator of the universe, and how great He is, but is based instead on the creature and his need to feel good. If we would do as Scripture says—to give to God our worship and praise—then a reciprocation would begin to take place. He would fill the very need we are crying out for. The great exchange takes place in our hearts in pure worship of Him and who He is.

I have heard many people say, "I don't hear from God." First, we must have some of Jesus formed in us in order to hear from God. Praise and worship is a good beginning for that to take place. We then have created a container within us that holds some of what Heaven has to pour out to us:

> ...*and they rest not day and night, saying Holy, holy, holy, Lord God Almighty, which was, and is, and is to come (Rev 4:8 KJV).*

This subject is very deep, but I just want to touch on it.

> *Draw near to God and He will draw near to you. Cleanse your hands, you sinners; and purify your hearts, you double-minded (James 4:8).*

Kingdom Keys

I have heard many people say, "I don't hear from God." ... There are various reasons why people do not hear from the Lord, but the most common is double mindedness.

We have two minds. One is our intellectual mind that is in our head, and the other is our heart mind that is in our innermost being. The Lord will speak to our heart mind. Sometimes we call it our gut feeling, but this is our "belly heart" which has its own mind. In our culture, people worship the intellect—the head mind—but the Lord teaches us through our inner heart mind. So, if you argue with your intellect vs. your heart, you are at war with yourself and the Lord. It does take trust to believe the inner voice, because this voice is very small. But we read that as sheep know the voice of their shepherd (John 10:14) you are assured you *will* hear the voice of the Lord if you belong to Him, and seek him with all your heart (mind).

We must learn to govern our intellectual thoughts, taking them captive and putting them under the Lordship of Jesus Christ. We must use the equipment that is given to us at salvation, even as a soldier is expected to wear the protective uniform and use the weaponry he is issued at enlistment. In doing this, we will find we are able to hear from the Lord. It will take the practice of quieting our intellectual minds to be able to hear that inner voice.

The Fountain of Love
April 20, 2008
In 2008, I saw a vision that I will try to describe to you. The vision was full of light, and I saw two tall, pencil-like angels about 20 feet tall with wings. Their

wings pointed backwards behind them, and they stood on either side of a beautiful fountain with stairs. The stairs were lit and there was water running softly down them. The water and the angels were completely illuminated. The angel on the right side of the fountain said, "My name is Hope," and, nodding toward the angel on the other side of the fountain, he continued, "and his name is Faith." Hope explained that the fountain had a name. It was called Love. He said, "Come, bathe in the Fountain of Love."

As I bathed, filthy things in my heart appeared on the surface of the water and then disappeared. I learned that an unloving heart is like dung in the spirit—it stinks, and others smell it as well. When we do not walk in love, people respond with bitterness. An unloving spirit gives the enemy a clear advantage over us, and sin prevails in our lives. From Heaven's perspective, most things that we look at on TV and speak in our conversations are filled with filth; they create a worldly sewer. Over time, we discover that doubt, fear, hopelessness, bitterness and resentment have begun to fill our hearts. Without realizing it, our lives have become like the sewer around us, filled with things that make us feel bad about ourselves and others. At times, we can even say life stinks. But when we bathe in the fountain of love, all that sewage melts away, and our cleansed lives become a sweet perfume, filled with the fragrance of God. I knew I needed to bathe more in His love for me and His love for others so that the sweet smells of Heaven would replace the stench of this world and its systems.

The angel called Hope had spoken to me, but Faith had not spoken. I was wondering why. Instantly, it was revealed that I could hear Hope's message because my life was full of the hope of receiving from God. I knew the Lord wanted to take me to a deeper level of believing Him. In order to converse with Faith, I needed the Faith of God. I had heavenly hope, but I did not have heavenly faith, so I could not hear Faith from this realm.

God was taking me on a journey beyond my earthly mind and natural circumstances. This realm was not filled with simple faith. It was filled with the "knowing God" kind of faith. Isaiah 55:9 says, *For as the heavens are higher than the earth, so are My ways higher than your ways, and My thoughts than your thoughts.* I needed to have the faith of Heaven in order to hear what the angel Faith had to say. I needed to break free of my carnal thoughts and have the mind of Christ. There was no condemnation or rejection from Faith. I felt only love.

We must first have hope, and hope will lead us to love—hoping that God loves us. When our spirits are filled with the love of God, knowing, rather than hoping, that He loves us, we will move on to the faith of God. When we have that perfect love, we know that we can do all things through Christ who strengthens us because He loves us. Perfect love casts out all fear. We know that because of God's love and compassion for others, we will have the faith of God to do what God is calling us to do. When we receive God's perfect love, we will be able to walk in perfect faith through that love. "The one who does not love does not know God, for God is love."

When we love, we start on the path to knowing God and we are able to move with Him. Everything God does, He does through love because He is love (1 John 4:8 NASB).

After the fountain of love, I saw a throne. Everything was brilliant. The atmosphere was golden and full of colors. God was on His throne and was surrounded by billions and billions of angels. He was giving the angels assignments, and they were going forth to fulfill their mission with a mandate from the throne room. God was sending them to do His will, and accomplish His purposes throughout the earth. The angels were going to help the saints.

Are not all angels ministering spirits sent to serve those who will inherit salvation? (Heb 1:14 NIV).

I knew that we had received many helpers from the Lord, and that He was sending help to others. Oh, that we would receive the provisions God has for us! But most of us think natural provision, not spirit provision. Yes, spirit provision will bring the natural provision too, but it is SO much more valuable.

We need help in these last days. I have heard of so many who lack understanding regarding angels interacting with us. Some reject the notion of angelic interaction outright, while others command them generically, without recognizing that—while on assignment to us—the angels are in submission to commands from the Throne. I am sure they have carried out much of what we have belched out in our decrees, simply because their function is to come alongside as a fellow minister to His will, in which we are doing our best to hit the mark. Unfortunately, religious spirits keep us from knowing the deeper truths of the Kingdom that are clearly seen in His Word, the Bible. We must have a believing heart to walk on kingdom ground. I understand now why Jesus wondered if He would find faith in the earth when He comes.

I am learning more about His ways and how His Kingdom works. I now understand why the Lord says He is the Lord of Hosts. The host of Heaven is mighty from the Lord for His people. Angels are neither for us nor against us, they are only for the Lord and for His will to be done on earth. They are not taken with human compassion nor can we persuade them. We cannot pray to them and ask them to do anything for us. For example, the angels that were given to me I do not pray to them to do anything. If I make a proclamation, I will do it as I am led by Lord Holy Spirit. Those helpers will do the work as the Father sees fit to send them into action. They are here to do the Father's bidding, and what He commands is absolute obedience to Him. They know exactly what the will of God is, and they carry it out without flinching.

Many times I have thought, "Oh, that I had a heart like that so that I would walk completely in obedience to His will. Then I would not succumb so easily to the 'good ole boys club', which honors man and his systems and does not see through the eyes of the spirit, but looks at the natural."

A long time ago, the Lord strongly admonished me, *"Stop looking at what your eyes can see, and instead, see with the eyes of the spirit."* It was an awesome word of correction for me. It changed my life because I have come to regularly check myself to make sure that I am not judging after the sight of my natural eyes. I seek the Lord to get His perspective. I look beyond "the smoke and mirrors" that the enemy so often holds up before my eyes.

The Lord's Training on Revival
April 28, 2008
Seymour and I were at a great revival. The meetings went on day and night; people were coming from all over the world to be touched by God. The church

was so overworked they needed help with everything. We volunteered to help in any area because we wanted to be a blessing to the church. We were given bathroom duty. Seymour cleaned the men's room and I cleaned the women's room. We did this the whole time we were there. The people who had been cleaning the bathrooms were so blessed because it gave them a break for a few days. They could go home earlier and rest.

After we finished cleaning the bathrooms, we asked if we could soak on the stage as they worshipped. The message that a minister gave earlier that day really stayed on my mind. As I lay there, I was thinking about the message, which was, "Walk in what his prophet has spoken," or, if we will walk in what the prophet has spoken, then we will receive the blessings of the Lord.

> *And they rose early in the morning, and went forth into the wilderness of Tekoa: and as they went forth, Jehoshaphat stood and said, Hear me, O Judah, and ye inhabitants of Jerusalem; Believe in the Lord your God, so shall ye be established; believe his prophets, so shall ye prosper (2 Chr 20:20).*

She spoke of faith, and not walking in doubt and unbelief. As I pondered her words, I saw transparent angels walking up and down the stage. One angel (who was not transparent) walked up to me. I could see only the bottom of his gleaming white robe. He said that I would do well if I listened to what was ministered. He stood there for a while, then he quietly took his place before me, where he proceeded to lie down and become part of me. I somehow knew the person who walked up to me was Jesus. I was learning to walk in transparency with Jesus. My heart needed to be open before Him, with no holding back or hiding of secret sins.

Impartations During Revival
April 29, 2008

Seymour was deep in worship. As he was worshiping, the pastor of the church we were attending looked at him and said, "The power of the Lord is all over this man—visions, dreams, and revelation." I was standing next to Seymour, and I saw a vision of us going up into a portal. The glory of the Lord was exceedingly powerful. Then, as I was about to hand the pastor a written copy of a vision I'd had of the revival angel, he said, "Take this back to your city from which you came. In the power that is in the revival, let it break out in Charleston, South Carolina."

I fell on the written copy of the vision and electricity filled my body. I then saw Jesus in color. His feet were brown, he had on a white robe, and I saw His bearded face. His body looked like it was presented on Venetian blinds. It was as if I were looking at Jesus' body on a set of open Venetian blinds set at an angle. His body was not yet one.

Steps of Understanding
(Interpretation):

My vision (walk with Jesus) was not quite clear. I knew that soon the Lord would make all things plain, but for now, I wasn't seeing Jesus as clearly as I should. This was training to see the body of Christ joined together to become one expression of Jesus and who He is.

Lying Spirits of Doubt During Revival
April 30, 2008

The Lord moved in awesome ways at a revival Seymour and I were attending. The following is our account.

A lot of people were in the prayer line. I could see the sicknesses in their bodies. As prayer went forth, healings simultaneously took place. I also heard the spirit of doubt and unbelief. He was like a person, and he was relentlessly causing unbelief to be solidly anchored in the hearts of the people to whom he spoke. The unbelief could not be stopped, even with clear evidence that people were being healed. I knew, even with irrefutable proof such as x-rays, unbelief would still be there.

This spirit was so strong that I could actually hear it speaking to me. It was telling me the people were joking or they were somehow coming up with their own healings, making people think they were getting healed. The only thing that broke the spirit of unbelief that was plaguing my mind was a deep hunger for God. Hunger and desperation broke the spirit of unbelief. If you want to receive what God has, you must break away from the spirit of doubt and unbelief. When you do, doubt and unbelief will disappear. "Lord, keep us hungry for You!" Seeking Jesus keeps our hearts tender so that we are always seeking His heart.

Before I won the battle of doubt and unbelief, I was challenging every healing in my mind. However, when I decided to get hungry, it left. It had no power over me; I wanted God. I praise God for this victory. I have to see the greater glory.

When I understood this, I was amazed that I could see people being healed. I could actually see the sicknesses in their bodies. I had to go through the battle of doubt and unbelief to get to the other side of faith (I believe this is another one of the helper angels that was named Faith). Hunger to see God move in His glory won the battle. It was as if the Lord opened my eyes to a new level.

One young child in line was autistic; the sickness was in his head. I saw the Spirit of the Lord, like a bright light in the shape of a flat disk move horizontally in the air in front of the boy's head, then move through his head. As this happened, the child was made completely whole. I watched the bright, golden light go into peoples' bodies as they were healed of all types of sickness. It was amazing! In others, I could see body parts being moved as the presence of Almighty God healed them. I was being trained to stand against doubting that comes when the Father moves.

The Currency of Heaven
April 30, 2008
I saw an angel with a bag of gold coins. A small angel gave them to me. I believe it was the currency of Heaven. Jesus spoke this:

"There is a new beginning for you and Seymour. You will walk in anointing, power, secrets revealed. Eyes more adjusted. You will walk with me. I am your Lord and Shepherd. Freedom, freedom is yours. No more religion for you. Breaking with the past. The past is over, no looking back at former things. A new day has begun for the both of you. I will show you the blueprints of your lives. Just follow the pattern laid out. It is simple, I will move through you. There will be a lot of quickening at My presence unfolding. Hope and Glory are yours, they will walk with you!"

The Lord had spoken: *Eyes more adjusted.* At this meeting, my eyes truly had been adjusted to see. The Lord was changing our value system.

> *How blessed is the man who finds wisdom And the man who gains understanding. For her profit is better than the profit of silver And her gain better than fine gold. She is more precious than jewels; And nothing you desire compares with her. Long life is in her right hand; In her left hand are riches and honor (Prov 3:13-16).*

Washing the Feet of the Body of Christ
May 1, 2008

In this vision, I was washing Jesus' feet and pens were given to me. I think this vision meant that I was washing the Body of Christ's feet and maybe this will be done through books. "*...so that He might sanctify her, having cleansed her by the washing of water with the word,*" (Eph 5:26, NASB). I trust that as you read, the Lord is writing a new chapter for your life in HIM! Let the writings on your heart before Him continue.

Chapter 9

Formed in the Spirit

May 11, 2008

I did not realize I had so much doubt in me until I began to see in the spirit. Days later I began to doubt that I saw Raphael and was unable to see him after that because of doubt.

Raphael was an angel of rank and to step here, I needed to believe God. I repented, and he appeared near the throne again, this time with a spear and a shield. This vision will be important later, because the Lord shows me what the thrones and spears do.

May 12, 2008

Often, where the Lord causes angels or objects to be placed in a vision are important. They speak of a coming authority. In this case, the Lord was saying this angel of rank would help in the execution of His authority in my life. I was out under the power, and I was pinned to the floor by the weight of His glory. I saw Raphael standing at my head.

May 13, 2008

I had a vision about a change of time in the earth. The Lord has given us the Keys to the Kingdom (*Matt. 16:19*). These truths that I see in pictures are throughout His Word. He was going to cause Seymour and me to open up a doorway of a change in His timing. The biblical books of Daniel and The Revelation speak of the changing of time.

I went up to Heaven and received another key. I saw an old lock, which was on a door. I put the key in the lock and opened it. But the lock held a door shut. I asked, "What is behind the door?" I heard: *TIME.* This vision is now coming to pass. Words that have been spoken by the prophets of old are now coming to pass. Scripture that has been sealed up for generations is coming forth. It is now time to see the hand of the Lord move upon mankind.

The glory of the Lord is going to cover the world as the waters cover the sea. This glory will not be as we suppose, but it will be in many forms—in blessings and in disasters. He roots up and plants anew. We are about see something from the Lord that has never been seen before. This is the time and this is the hour for the winding down of the evil that man has made in the earth.

The Natural Man Cannot Receive the Things of God

I was looking in the spirit and I saw a papier mache' man that had a big blocky head with square arms, legs, and body. He was like a shapeless cutout. I heard the Lord identify him as the "natural man." The Adamic nature has no form, and has no understanding of the ways of God. When we are saved and do not let the Lord's ways be formed in us, then our spiritual walk has no form or dimension— no eyes with which to see, no hands with which to reach out, and no feet with which to walk. The Lord was saying He was forming Seymour's and my spiritual walk so we could move from the natural man to the spiritual man. The natural man cannot receive the things of the Spirit *(1 Cor 2:14).*

The "natural man" is without form and unable to function, as he cannot receive the things of the spirit

May 25, 2008

We were at a worship service at our local church. I saw that God was anointing a generation to go through perilous times. The anointing is so we are not overwhelmed and so that we will know the Father is with us. I know that God will anoint a generation to go through what must take place, just as the Lord anointed the early church to go through persecution. We need not fear or be afraid because the Father will be with us.

This generation will need this anointing because the majority of this generation is weak—emotionally, physically, and socially. The Lord sends His anointing to cause us to do the impossible. In the natural, this generation is not like former generations that had family values and a strong moral compass. Without this foundation, one cannot be successful when times are tough and still keep a moral standard. Instead, this generation can easily become as animals, with the survival of the fittest since they do not know hardship, they only know comfort. Anything that is needed is just a store away. It will take anointing to give what they do not possess.

> *And I heard a great voice in Heaven, saying, Now is come the salvation, and the power, and the kingdom of our God, and the authority of his Christ: for the accuser of our brethren is cast down, who accuseth them before our God day and night. And they overcame him because of the blood of the Lamb, and because of the word of their testimony; and they loved not their life even unto death. Therefore rejoice, O heavens, and ye that dwell in them. Woe for the earth and for the sea: because the devil is gone down unto you, having great wrath, knowing that he hath but a short time (Rev 12:10-12 ASV).*

May 26, 2008

I was in prayer and soaking when I had a vision of myself kneeling in front of Raphael. He had a sword and brought the sword down once on each shoulder. It was as though I were being knighted. I had on a beautiful, one-piece white dress with diamonds all over it.

Chapter 10

Sending Forth

May 26, 2008

The Lord said, "Perilous times are coming on the earth. My deliverance and judgment will be over my people. Preparing a way for this earth to be judged will be over my people. Strong delusion will be over them because they refuse to see what I am doing. Men's hearts will fear. But you move on. Don't fear. Just speak My Word, whether it is received or not.

I showed you the four rivers of refreshing. All those who will be refreshed will have the River of Life. The others will come when their testings are over. Those who drink will have peace. Those who don't will be stressed for a time, until they believe me and walk after me. The harvest is ripe. Laborers are going, and the face of the Church will change to a more radical church. They will believe Me and begin walking in My Word. Generational curses will not hold them back. They will be set free because they hungered for Me and Me alone."

June 5, 2008

I received the following word from the Lord:

"These are new days for you. I have roared at your enemies. Bright things are coming for you; they are even here now. Rise up and rejoice, you shall see the long-awaited plan. You have passed your testing, now see the salvation of your God. Everything in you shall

*turn around. New "suddenlies" will come, too. You are blessed of God. Go, and do my
exploits. They are resident in you; I have put them there. Prepared works set into it. Just*

Kingdom Keys

The Warrior Bride really does do war, with HIS weapons of
choice. In this instance, righteously clothed and jeweled,
bedecked with the ability to house HIS light and translate
Heaven's sendings into HIS shining glories.

*step into it; don't fear. Arise, beloved of God, and go from here and do the works of
God. Fear not! I have given you the city. You are protected, just rest in My Word and
in My strength. You have orders and a mandate. Go!"*

A couple was staying at the same house we were during a revival we
were attending. A friend from England asked us to pray and give them the
gift of spiritual sight. The Lord had said I could give to those who are hungry
and who have open hearts. (In order to receive anything from the Lord
you must be hungry; a closed heart will not receive anything).

Sue had never before seen in the spirit. We prayed and she saw mountains in
the distance. During the service later, she continued to see the same vision.
She saw eagles flying high around a mountain. She told us it was the Mountain
of the Lord, and Seymour and I were the eagles. We were watching the
Mountain of the Lord, and for a time we were hidden. We broke off our beaks
and sucked water from the rock, we were being rejuvenated, after we were
renewed, we flew high, very high. Few could fly that high, but we were seeing
the streams and special things that no one else could see, and we were letting
others know what the Lord was saying and what was going on in the spirit.

The Fear of the Lord

In prayer, I immediately felt the presence of the Lord. It came to me differently this time, and I felt the fear of the Lord. This fear was so great that every cell within my body began to vibrate with His presence. I shook from the inside out with the fear of the Lord. I knew I needed to obey him on every conscious level.

This was not about being afraid. It was the deep reverence due a holy God. I would never forget this experience. The fear of the Lord imprinted itself upon my very being; I knew I had to respect the Lord. I needed to obey him because he is the great I AM. I felt the awesome power of God—how little we are, and how great He is! Nevertheless, He delights in spending time with me. When we know the fear of the Lord, we will not dishonor Him. We will not take him for granted, but will understand that He is the great and mighty God that we serve.

June 26, 2008

I saw myself dancing. (It is a vision I have had many times.) I am dancing with someone on my left and someone on my right. Suddenly, I was taken to a new level of worship. Twirling ribbons all around me propelled me up to a new level. I saw myself traveling over water. I was then in Peru, and I walked the streets and came to an old woman's home. She was lying on the floor. Suddenly, snakes appeared. At the same time, a flaming sword appeared in my hand. I killed the snakes in the woman's room, and she was healed.

I traveled over the water again to another place. I saw a man in chains; I took my sword and cut the man's head off. (Cutting the head off symbolizes cutting off a person's authority. The Lord wants to take our minds out of the equation. He wants us to have the mind of Christ instead. Our will/authority is a part of our mind.) I cut the shackles off of his legs. The one on his left leg was a little difficult to break. When it was finally broken off, Jesus washed him in the water.

Then I saw myself, and a gold and red necklace with a book on it was given to me. The necklace was made of pearls and the book that hung from the pearls was gold and red. The book would change to a heart and back to a book. I said, "Lord, I just want to be with you." Then I saw a beautiful garden that was so green! As I walked past flowers in the garden, they bloomed to give me impartation. I was with Jesus and the Holy Spirit and the Father. (I just want to be with Him!)

Chapter 11

Acceleration

July 1, 2008
As I woke up, I heard: ***ACCELERATION!***

Anson Street

Many times, throughout my book, you will read about a place called Anson Street. I am referring to St. John's Reformed Episcopal Church located on Anson Street in Charleston, SC. This is where the Lord assigned us to pray. We were led by the Lord to join other believers who had just started praying there on Tuesday mornings.

At that time, we did not know the significance of Anson Street. Later, we found out that in 1857, just before the Civil War, black and white believers sought the Lord there for a spiritual awakening, and God showed up. From their prayers, a revival window was opened in the heavens. In 1858, this revival reached New York and later swept across the United States, and one million people were saved.

The second time we went to pray at Anson Street, I heard the Lord say, "Go down to the front and kneel before me." When I knelt, the angel of the Lord suddenly appeared in glowing, brilliant white attire with a burgundy-red sash from his left shoulder to his right hip. He said, "I am the Revival Angel of Charleston." He had a glowing glass bowl in his hands filled with swirling blue and magenta incense. He offered the bowl to me. It was a key. Then the angel said, "Take the key and open the door." I reached out physically and took the bowl. Then the angel said, "The floodgates will open to you. Be bold as a lion. I am with you. I will flood the city. I will push back the opposition. We have been waiting for someone to open the gate. Open the gates that will flood the city. Must be pure in heart; worship is the key. No agendas. Just worship, pure worship."

He continued, "I am the Revival Angel of this city. This [church at Anson Street] is the seat of revival in this city. Open the gates. Open the gates." I was afraid, because I had watched people's lives being destroyed as they interceded for this city. He went on, "You are hidden. Don't fear. Don't fear man or his heart, I will flood the city. Many will gain hope for a new future. Some destruction will take place. But I will rebuild what is ruined."

I cried, "Help me, strengthen me!" He responded strongly, "You are strengthened! This IS the hour and time. Don't fear. Go forth…the time is at hand. This is the hour. You are blessed."

He repeated, "You are strengthened. This IS the hour and time. Don't fear. Go forth…the time is at hand. This is the hour. You are blessed."

It is interesting to note that Philip Simmons, the master blacksmith who fashioned most of the iron gates throughout Charleston and beyond, attended this church most of his life. Known as a humble man with a big heart, he died toward the end of our time at Anson Street. How I appreciate God's pictures set in place for us to see.

The key given in the vision were not like our idea of keys. The key was actually a glowing bowl filled with swirling blue and magenta incense, which represented pure worship and prayer. He instructed me that "pure" worship is worship without an agenda. When he handed me the key in the spirit, I physically grabbed it to bring it into the natural.

I got up from the altar to return to my seat. I heard in the spirit, "Get up and worship." Our friend B.J. was leading worship, and I did not want to override his authority. He was singing about Israel. Just as I was wondering what to do, B.J. fell over sideways onto the floor with his guitar and I heard, "Get up and sing." I obeyed.

Then Seymour said, "Let's get in the rotunda and form a circle." When we did, the angel said, "Now stir the waters." So I did a parabolic act (a natural act that has spiritual implications and weight and rule before the Lord). For example, Ezekiel the prophet was told by the Lord to eat his food over dung and lay on his side to show Israel their sins. Also, the act of swirling the waters using Seymour's burgundy Bible. *The Lord was saying to us with this act that the Word would be living springs in us. The waters of life that are in the Word were coming forth from His throne.*

Twice, I did a whirlwind action up from the waters of the pool. While I was doing this, the hand of the angel who gave me the bowl was touching my back. Suddenly, the Spirit of the Lord fell, and everyone began to prophesy. I had not told anyone of my experience. They began saying the very words that the revival angel had spoken to me. I felt a bursting, like water gushing through me. It came from my back and burst out of my chest.

July 12, 2008
I was praying in the spirit. The Lord put a bluish shield of faith on my heart. Etched in the shield was the word, *Faith.* I saw two large white eagles standing back to back. Their tail feathers were creating a whirlwind.

July 16, 2008
I saw a crystal city. Then I touched a Seraph. The Seraph looked like a lion with hair like silk. I touched his fur with my fingers, and my fingers turned gold.

Training on the Spirits of Deception
July 22, 2008
Early morning, I awoke and saw chariots of fire and a host of angels. This was Tuesday, the day we participated in prayer for revival at Anson Street. As I sat in the church, I had a deceiving vision. In the vision, an angel of light walked up to me with a scowl on his face. He took the bowl from me as if I had done something wrong and was being punished. He turned and walked away from me. Then I looked down and saw the bowl still sitting in my lap. He could not take the bowl from me because He did not give it to me. The Lord gave it to me. He could only try to make me believe he had taken it.

I realized I had just seen a deceiver. I believe the Lord showed me this so that I might learn about the spirit of deception and how deceiving spirits operate by making you feel you are always doing something wrong and falling short; making you feel condemned and that you are not doing what God has called you to do. And that God is going to take away what He has freely given. I learned that the enemy couldn't take away what the Lord has freely given. He was trying to get me to act in a spirit of unbelief and not operate where the Lord just put me. The Lord said, *Get up and sing*, so I did. Then the presence of the Lord fell on everyone there.

The Lord would teach me many things about the spirit of deception. The Lord taught me how he operates, how he loves to bring confusion and division. I learned he extracts worship for himself. He leads people away from the heart of God and out of the peace of God. I learned that if you are going to walk in the things of God, you must have the heart of God.

Years later, the Lord would speak to me this phrase, "Don't make a move until the Father speaks to you." If we move outside of His speaking, we will find ourselves on the enemy's ground, where the enemy operates. This was a very important training time for me to learn how not to be deceived. The Lord does not move in fear, but teaches us faith.

Earlier in the book, I spoke of the four levels of spirits that try to bind us and that we must master them. At the beginning of my walk with the Lord, He showed me a bride standing at a church altar. She was looking up at the Lord. She was beautiful, and her dress more exquisite than any gown a bride could hope to wear. Her veil was made up of crowns upon crowns that went up about five feet, with the veil and the train of her dress flowing halfway down the aisle.

On the back row of the church was a bag lady. She had a dirty rag upon her head and was surrounded by dirty bags, to which she held tightly. Jesus appeared in the middle of the aisle and He said these words to me, "You can be the beautiful bride, or you can be the bag lady." The Bride completely followed the Lord's leading and kept her eyes on Jesus (i.e. continuously looking up) while the bag lady kept her focus on her bags of clothes. They were filled with her past, things she had stuffed away but kept close to her no matter how much they rotted or smelled.

I understood that both of these people were a picture of me. The one that sin made (the bag lady) and the one that God made (the bride). I screamed, "Lord, I want to be the bride!" At that moment, I was meeting the Revival Angel of Charleston. I knew I had finally let the work of the Lord be completed in me. I was able to move to a whole new level in the Lord, and I was no longer carrying the low level personal stuff. I had conquered enough of self-life to be able to work with the greater princes that the Lord had established over the region of Charleston. I still had to conquer faithlessness and a doubting spirit. I had learned the secret of these words.

July 25, 2008

A guest minister was at a local church that we were attending. He prayed for everyone there. When he prayed for us, he said, "Charleston filled with the Holy Ghost." I fell out under the power of God and began to laugh uncontrollably. I saw the bowl that the revival angel gave me open. (I thought to myself, *How can a bowl open? Is this part of its changing form?*) This time, it changed into a megaphone. Now the incense had direction.

Every Friday we would pray at Anson Street, and the Lord began to speak to me about blessing the city. So during prayer, we would sing the song of a blessing over Charleston. The direction that the Lord gave us was to pray for God's original design over the city of Charleston.

We would speak whatever scriptures the Lord led us to speak over the city. People would say they could hear the song of the Lord ringing over the city, ten blocks away from the church. The Lord was saturating the city with His sound.

Chapter 12

Training Us in the Precious

July 26, 2008

Moreover, I will make your battlements of rubies, And your gates of crystal, And your entire wall of precious stones (Isaiah 45:12).

I saw a new day and a field. When I looked closely at what was in the field, I saw jewels growing. First, I saw diamonds growing, then rubies and sapphires and other precious stones. They were growing in patches. I began to walk on the jewels. When I saw jewels in this vision, I knew the Lord was teaching me how to handle the precious things of the kingdom, "pearls of great price." We were walking and experiencing the holy and precious things that the Lord holds dear to his heart. We were moving in what the Lord wanted to operate in. We were desirous no matter the cost. Many times we did not understand why the Lord called us to pray every Friday at Anson Street. Nevertheless, we were willing to stand and hold the ground because He said we should do this. No matter what size crowd, I would speak what I heard from the Lord on Friday. By Tuesday or Wednesday, we would see the word fulfilled.

July 27, 2008

A scroll was handed to me, and I took it. On the scroll was written, *It is written.* Also, I saw a wing in gold that was like a protective covering over the scroll. The Lord was uncovering the hidden Word to us. What has been written for generations had been hidden for ages. The Lord was going to uncover His written words in a new and different way.

> *And he said unto me, These words are faithful and true: and the Lord, the God of the spirits of the prophets, sent his angels to show unto his servants the things which must shortly come to pass (Rev 22:6).*

July 30, 2008

For several days, at midnight, I saw chariots of fire. A band of angels followed the chariots. This was the same vision I saw the first time Seymour and I went to Anson Street, but this day I saw myself riding in the chariot. Before riding in the chariot, both Seymour and I saw a crystal city. I saw a locked, golden door. I discovered I had the key, so I opened the golden door and saw treasures—gold, diamonds, and jewels. At first, it was like walking into a room without lights, yet I could see the treasure. Then a glowing, bright light was turned on and I could see everything clearly. I looked and thought, "We need supplies to help people during perilous times, and we need funds for land and a building."

August 08, 2008

I was lying in water and breathing it in. I then saw an open Bible which became light and fire. I had on a beautiful dress. Words from the Bible came out and began to appear on the dress. They were dressing me for what would come.

I have since learned that the Lord wants us to walk in the Word to such a degree that we become like Jesus. We are living Bibles so that if people do not read the Word, they should be able to look at us and see the word of God in action, living and breathing through vessels that fully belong to Him. Jesus said, "The works I do, you shall do greater." I believe He is the Word walked out among men and women; we must be in this earth looking and acting like Jesus.

September 07, 2008

As I was lying down before the Lord, I saw the River of Life. I took a drink. A butterfly flew over my head and then turned into a book. Gold dust came out of the book and fell over my head. I could physically feel the gold dust falling on my head. Then I saw a key. I thought, "Another key?" The key was taken and put into my heart. My heart opened and gifts were put in. Then I quietly remained there in the River of Life.

When we rest in the Lord, meditating on God's Word (the River of Life), the troubles and heaviness of this world (i.e. my authority, which is the heaviness of my trying to be in control) become light (the butterfly), letting God lead the way. The Word goes in deeper and we have a greater understanding of His Way. There is an impartation (gold dust) for holy thoughts.

Kingdom Keys

There is no path like HIS Path. If He be for us, it does not matter if the whole world is against us. It would be us and God against whomever. The whomevers are ALWAYS the minority, no matter how large their numbers or supposed strengths.

This is a great impartation, and it is the key to removing from the heart all doubt and unbelief. The Word opens our hearts, and the gifts that were created for us before the foundation of the world are imparted to us and become active.

We must learn to dwell in the River of God and enter into the rest of the Lord. In this vision, the Lord was showing me the key to walking with the Lord—resting in the Lord and thinking about Jesus. It opens our hearts and minds to His will for our lives.

And he showed me a pure river of water of life, clear as crystal, proceeding out of the throne of God and of the Lamb (Rev 22:1).

Afterward he measured a thousand; and it was a river that I could not pass through; for the waters were risen, waters to swim in, a river that could not be passed through (Ezek 47:5).

Chapter 13

The Hour of Testing

Beloved, do not be surprised at the fiery ordeal among you, which comes upon you for your testing, as though some strange thing were happening to you; (1 Pet 4:12).

Future Things to Come
October 3, 2008

It was a month before the presidential elections; I was feeling a little lost. We were at a church and the organization, Women of Action, was having a soaking school. I was lying down on a bench, praying and seeking God about various things, when I saw myself in a beautiful garden (the old people used to call it the Garden of Prayer. Many songs have been written about it).

There was a beautiful waterfall in the garden. With my natural ears, I heard the water hitting the water below the fall. I saw Jesus come over to me, so tender in spirit. There appeared a small puddle of water about 2 to 4 inches deep between Him and me. I looked deep into the puddle as Jesus moved the water with His right hand, and I saw our master bedroom and den. The renovation on these rooms was completed. He moved the water again, and I saw a large bomb go off. It was very plain. Then I saw John McCain's face in the bomb. I was wondering who would be our next president after Bush. The choice was between Barack Obama and John McCain. I think God was saying McCain was not ready.

He moved the water again and I saw men, women and children standing in lines. They were dressed in old clothes. Jesus moved the water one more time, and I saw large animals like cows die. The birds were eating the bodies. President Obama was elected. The following are news reports after he took office:

Nov. 19, 2009, CNBC: According to the government's broadest measure of unemployment, some 17.5 percent are either without a job entirely or underemployed. The so-called U-6 number is at the highest rate since becoming an official labor statistic in 1994.

Dec. 21, 2009, CNBC: "We're seeing many more people from the middle class than we've ever seen before," said Elizabeth Quackenbush, Chief Development Officer for Harvest Hope Food Bank. "People who used to donate are now standing in line for food. People who are unemployed and underemployed. People trying hard to make ends meet, having two, maybe three jobs. More professional people who've been laid off and have overcome the shame often associated with going to a food bank to ask for food. It's not a pretty picture."

Jan. 16, 2009 (AP) Drought conditions in Texas are so bad cattle are keeling over in parched pastures and dying.

November 17, 2008

I saw the eye of the Lord on a person that was kneeling and praying before Him. The person was weeping and repenting of their sins; truly repenting from their heart. As this person was repenting to the Father, a bright spotlight came down on him. Suddenly, rainbow-colored light exploded in all directions like a supernova over this person's life, completely dissolving the darkness of sin around them.

When we repent, we understand that God is more important than we are. When we just feel bad about ourselves and our focus is on ourselves instead of God, we are not truly repenting. We are saying we are more important than the Lord. Instead of repentance, it is the pride of self-preservation. Self-preservation is preserving self and our self-focused interests rather than stepping out of self and wanting to see and know who God is. All the creatures and the elders in Heaven see and understand that He is holy. Once we understand that He is holy, and call out in a heart of repentance, His eye will turn to us and heal us.

November 8, 2008

We were at Anson Street, and the Lord had me read Revelation through all seven seals. It was very powerful. We all felt the presence of God, which moved mightily in the church. We all had a sense of awe.

It started when I saw the Angel of the Lord, the Revival Angel of Charleston, and Jesus all standing behind me as I led worship. I was looking through Scripture, because I wanted to share something that would encourage us all. Instead, I found myself reading Revelation 4, 5, and 6 about the Throne of Heaven and those around the Throne crying, "Holy, Holy, Holy." Afterwards I read about the book no one could open, and then on through the seven seals. It was not at all encouraging, nevertheless, as I read I saw that the Father would make known who are His and who are not. I prayed that I would be found to be His.

After I read, I saw a white path coming from Heaven to earth. The Lord was coming on it; He was on a horse and there were horses with riders following Him. He was coming as the King. (The Lord was standing behind me this whole time as the glowing Shepherd.) I was compelled to write this vision.

December 2008

I was sad and discouraged because I did not see the promise. I saw Raphael. He glowed and touched my heart, and I felt better.

The promises were the things that the Lord had so abundantly spoken of all the months earlier. I was being a microwave believer; I wanted everything to happen in a few months. I did not understand that the Lord had to prepare my heart and my soul to receive the things He had spoken me.

December 6, 2008

I was praying, and I was handed a white glowing scroll. It said: *HOPE FOR A FUTURE.*

Chapter 14

Times of Preparation

January 1, 2009

I saw myself on a wheel with the angel of the Lord and Jesus. We were spinning, and there was a whirling wind all around us. I think this vision meant that even though I was fleshly in some of my ways, the Spirit was still leading me. The wheel represented the moving of the Spirit.

> *Wherever the spirit was about to go, they would go in that direction. And the wheels rose close beside them; for the spirit of the living beings was in the wheels (Ezek 1:20 NASB).*

January 2, 2009

Our church fasted for 21 days. It was easy because the Lord was with us. Everyone was asked to fast something. Some fasted coffee, TV, chocolate or whatever they wanted to give the Lord. I went on a liquid fast and prayed, "Lord, I don't want any more wasted time in my life." I wanted to be God-controlled and God-led, yielding my will to the Father. I wanted to be taken over by Jesus and the Holy Spirit—no more self-life with me in control.

The Lord spoke: "I am going to awaken something new and fresh in you and Seymour. The days of suffering and hardship are over. My ways will be clear and plain. "Rousing" will come and be a blessing to all who hear my words of encouragement. Freedom will come to my people, encouraging words and overcoming thoughts. All obstacles are now removed from you so you can go forth with vigor and power in My might. In blessing, I will bless. In healing, I will heal you. You are mine and greatly loved by the Father and me. The word of the Lord that will be given into your hands is important."

> *Proclaim this among the nations: Prepare a war; rouse the mighty men! Let all the soldiers draw near, let them come up! Beat your plowshares into swords And your pruning hooks into spears; Let your weak say, "I am a mighty man." Hasten and come, all you surrounding nations, And gather yourselves there. Bring down, O LORD, Your mighty ones. Let the nations be aroused. And come up to the valley of Jehoshaphat. For there I will sit to judge All the surrounding nations. Put in the sickle, for the harvest is ripe. Come, tread, for the wine press is full; The vats overflow, for their wickedness is great. Multitudes, multitudes in the valley of decision! For the day of the Lord is near in the valley of decision (Joel 3:9-14 NASB).*

January 17, 2009

Mahesh Chavda was in Charleston. During the service, I saw about 200 angels, dancing and having fun. They were over the worship team. This reminds me of another vision I had four or five years earlier.

We were at Mahesh Chavda's meeting in Charlotte, NC with a friend of ours. I saw a large angel standing behind Seymour and me. He had a candle in his left hand and an antique box in his right hand. His wings were open wide as though he were covering us. I told no one. I thought I was seeing things. Seymour and I went down for prayer. After the prayer, we went down on our knees, crying out to God and asking Him to please help us. Mahesh came over to us because we were the only ones left and we were kneeling and praying. He prayed for us and then said, "You are leaving here with an angel." I was so surprised. I had not mentioned the angels I was seeing. It is so wonderful when God confirms what He is showing so that we will believe. We were also told God was sending us to Russia (which God did do to strengthen the churches there.)

Many times I saw this angel with the antique box in his hand. I would see the box open and things would come out of the box. Some of the things I saw were vines, flowers, and gold dust. Later there were manifestations of gold dust falling in the church—gold, silver and rainbow colored. When a flower appeared, we grew numerically. When I saw the vines, people were getting healed from sicknesses; some were healed of AIDS, cancer, and paralysis from strokes. One lady came with her child who had a shattered bone in his arm. He was to get an operation the next day and would have to have pins in his arm. The Lord gave him a new bone. The following Sunday she gave the testimony that he did not have surgery. Praise the Lord, God is still healing His people.

February 6, 2009

I saw someone in white, dancing. I did not see her face. What was important was the dress—white and seamless with a rope for a belt. She danced beautifully. As I watched, the belt changed color. First it was light blue, then gold, then red, and then dark blue. She kept dancing and suddenly, the four colors were woven together and the belt became about four inches thick. It went around her waist in a herringbone pattern. Seymour said they were the colors of the curtains where the Ark of the Covenant was kept.

Steps of Understanding
(Interpretation):

Keep looking up and let Jesus form you. Hear and obey, and let Him take the lead. I was becoming the Bride, able to be dressed as He wanted to dress me. As you will see later, being dressed in revival clothes was part of the angel's job, given to those who were willing to put on the robes he was offering to us all.

February 13, 2009

All day, I saw angels carrying crates of various things. I told Seymour what I saw and he said, "What has been stored up and not used is put in crates." I saw the crates being delivered during worship at Anson Street. I asked the Lord what was happening in the atmosphere around me. Then I saw someone putting huge shoes on me. They were about fifty times bigger than my feet.

Then I saw a white rope rolling down from the sky over me. Right in front of me, I saw a huge angel wearing a simple white dress with a soft touch of yellow in it. He was standing out on the peninsula of Charleston with one foot on part of the land and one foot on the other part of the land. The angel was looking toward Charleston. He had a lightning bolt in his left hand, and a scale in his right hand. On the left part of the scale were five loaves of bread with a napkin over them. On the other side of the scale, I saw a cup of wine and a cup of oil.

February 26, 2009

All day yesterday I was in a complaint mode, about us not growing (our local church) our visions being many, but not much fruit in the form of crowds and strong church attendance. The next day, one of our church members said, "What if all that God has spoken was not going to happen; would God be enough? If what we have is all we're going to have; would He be enough for us?" I had to settle in my spirit that God would be enough for us, and it brought me peace.

As I worshipped on the 26th, I was in a throne room. A cry went up out of my spirit, "Jesus, have mercy and grace over us!!" Instantly, I was taken from that throne room to another one. There was smoke and a rainbow over the throne and living creatures. As I stood there I heard the word, "BELIEEEEEEEEEEEEEVE!!!!" The only way I can describe what I heard is that it was a continual, echoing sound. It was like the Word says in Revelation 14:2, "And I heard a voice from Heaven, like the sound of many waters..." The sound of the word "believe" went on and on and on, yet, it was spoken only one time.

Then, instantly, I was in a different throne room that looked like a courtroom. The room was huge, and the court was in the shape of a cone, like an amphitheater. There were throne-like chairs and there where people sitting on them. I could not see who they were. I was at the bottom on the floor of this theater looking upward. There were many thrones that formed the cone. In the center, at the bottom, there were two thrones on the floor. I was standing on the floor near the two thrones. A scepter was handed out to me. I reached out for it, and my hand went inside the scepter. It was like reaching into soft, blue water.

The scepter was golden and the end of the scepter was blue. I had the thought that since I was there, I could cry out for mercy and take a moment to plead my case. To my surprise, instead of "mercy" coming out of my mouth, I shouted, "Grace, grace!" My spirit was shouting grace so that the judgment over us would be grace.

Then I was carried back to the throne room with the single throne and the rainbow and smoke. A creature that looked like a lion walked over to me like a cat approaching a person to show affection. I had seen him before. When I rubbed his back, gold came off onto my hands. This lion had eyes all over its body. I realized while I was touching the lion that I had touched one of his eyes. From this one touch, eyes appeared on my hand and went up my arm.

While I was in the vision, Seymour touched my left hand, the hand with the eyes. When he did, I saw eyes begin to go up his right arm. I touched my eyes so I could see greater. I was able to see in the spirit with greater and greater insight. The eyes appeared to give sight. My sight grew when they touched me. While I was in the throne room with the rainbow, I saw a tall, slender, black angel. I sensed he was accusing me. Then I saw him shrink to the size of a small soccer ball.

That night, I awoke at 4:24 am, and I saw an angel standing at the foot of my bed, snapping a tape measure. I heard the words: "Arise and measure, for all time has come up before me. CRY MERCY, for the whirling wheels have started to turn." The wheels were moving in a forward direction. I was told to pay attention to the time. Then the vision ended.

Chapter 15

Everything is Changing

May 8, 2009

While at Anson Street, I saw lights that looked like the Northern Lights in Alaska. The lights were over everyone in the church. Then I saw Jesus. He was beautiful, dressed in a white robe with multicolored jewels around the chest. He wore a thin crown on His head. He was dressed for a wedding, but His clothing looked comfortable. During the vision, we (the people at Anson Street) were singing about the wedding. Jesus came and washed my feet and put me on a golden path. He began to walk down the path in front of me and told me to follow Him, so I did. As we were leaving, I heard a reminder to write down my visions. As I sat down to sing, I saw an angel that was 40′ tall. The bowl of prayer inside me glowed and turned into a whirlwind as I sang. It opened doors in the spirit. I saw an army coming out in full armor. I heard the same thing I had heard in other visions −"Change; everything is changing."

God has been working in us since we started praying at Anson Street. The prayers are being worked in and out and through us. The work is big and powerful. We are being built with overcoming power and strength so that we can move with God. The power and strength will enable us to move from being comforted to being empowered.

June 4, 2009

The Lord said, "The change is coming." I found the Lord would speak to me the same things over and over again. When He did this He was preparing me to be ready for what He was speaking. This is what was happening here.

June 5, 2009

I saw a scene of Israeli boys with black hats and curls falling down on their faces. There were also men and women in the scene, all in distress. The boys were pulling the dust over their heads and moaning. The women were crying. I saw them being mowed down with guns, there were bombs falling everywhere.

June 8, 2009

I saw obese people being denied food and support from the government because of their weight. They were in concentration-type camps. Thin people were in one camp and overweight people were in another. I saw this vision many times; it was as if there was not enough food to feed the people. I wondered what would happen when they lost the weight—would they be taken out of these camps?

June 12, 2009

At 4:46 am, I awoke to see a vision of a raging fire with black smoke. It was the aftermath of an explosion.

June 23, 2009

I saw a silver path to walk on; silver represents redemption. The Lord was beginning to redeem some things in the earth. Later, while in prayer, I saw a wall of water with wood and debris in it. I saw a map of the East coast near or around the outer banks of North Carolina. Later that day, I saw a casket moving down the road in a vision. It was someone that the world knew, because it was a worldwide funeral. I also had the sense it was a black man. Two days later, on June 25, 2009, Michael Jackson died.

July 3, 2009

I saw the USA and a fire was burning across it like a piece of paper burns from one side to the other. I had the sense it was traveling across the land from the east coast to the west coast. The fire stopped one third of the way.

July 8, 2009

I was going for a walk and I smelled a terrible smell. I heard the Lord say, *"It is a spirit."* Then all that day I smelled it off and on. I was being trained by the Lord.

July 9, 2009

I awoke and wondered what was going on. The Lord told me that He was showing me strategies of the enemy. I saw a sword and a great light slash a spirit.

That same day, I saw what looked like trillions of American dollars. The money was on pallets. There were two or three of them. The pallets had wheels and were similar to the flatbed carts at Sam's Club used to carry large amounts of food and supplies. There were men wheeling the pallets into a vault, and they wore tan uniforms with a circular patch on their arm. The circular patches were traced in red and had a hammer inside.

July 24, 2009

I was ministering in worship at Anson Street, and I saw a line drawn in the sand. Those who believed were on the right side of the line and those who put the Lord in a box were on the left side of the line. The ones on the left had built an image of the Lord—not a true image but one that they were comfortable with and able to handle. The way on the left side of the line was called "unbelief." I also heard the words, "Civil War in the church." I knew the war was between those who believe and those who do not.

Then I said, "Where is the Angel of the Lord?" (I was referring to the revival angel at Anson Street.) He came forward and threw out the contents of the first bowl. It contained the prayers the Lord had told us to pray and the scriptures He wanted us to read over the city and the nation. As the contents came out of the bowl, it was thick and blue in color. The substance grew and became like a river. The blue meant communion and relationship. Surely this was true; we had been learning keys of intimacy at Anson Street. There was also a light blue which meant will and perseverance. We have had to persevere to keep going to Anson Street every Friday night. *(No other but Your will be done, Oh Lord!)*

As the angel threw the blue bowl, I was immediately handed a second bowl. It was a clear bowl with red incense in it. According to some vision reference books, red means cords of wisdom, anointing and power. *(Oh dear Lord, give us the anointing!)*

The Lord had me read Ezekiel 17 (the parable of two eagles, a vine and Zedekiah's rebellion) then Ezekiel 12:22, ("Son of man, what is this proverb you people have concerning the land of Israel, saying, 'The days are long and every vision fails'?)" then Ezekiel 10 (vision of God's glory departing from the temple).

August 14, 2009

At Anson Street, I saw Seymour and myself clothed in jewels. We had a crown of gold and jewels, a robe of white and a tunic covered in jewels. The jewels went down the front and around the neckline and around the cuffs of the robes. The jewels were royal blue, red and white. They were beautiful.

August 28, 2009

In a vision at Anson Street, I heard the Lord say, "I am here." People were saying, "Have you ever seen anything like this?" Everyone was shocked. It was the Day of the Lord. I saw the Revival Angel of Charleston, who came and stood inside Seymour and me. Later, during worship, the angel put his hand on the back of my head and I saw the throne room of the Lord. Seymour saw two tall angels at the back of the church. One was pouring water, and the other was pouring wheat.

September 9, 2009

As we prayed in home group, I asked everyone to set their hearts on the Lord and think on Him. As I prayed, a ladder went up to Heaven and the angel, Sally, was there. She said, "Hurry." I saw fruit in a wheelbarrow. The fruit was big, red, and perfect.

I saw Pogo, who said, "Don't worry, I'll carry you over." Then I saw Raphael, and he was practicing with a spear. The Tree of Life appeared; it was a beautiful scene. Jesus was there and He said simply, *"Believe."*

I saw disturbances, but a glass bubble was protecting the people of God. Some people in the bubble had their faces against the glass staring out at what was going on; they were afraid and did not understand they were protected. Others walked around unmoved by the devastation; they're the ones who believed God.

December 11, 2009

We were at Anson Street. One of the sisters wrote the following words as they were spoken. The Lord said, "These are the days of tribulation. Be a fire that burns. Be kindling. Set your eyes upon the Lord like never before. Don't be worried. Be prepared soldiers of the King, forgiving every transgression. You must not have a wound that the enemy can stick a sword in. Prepare like never before; this is a time for preparation. The mighty ones will arise. *KNOW ME! KNOW ME!* Many exploits will come forth. Many storms. Don't think natural. Many storms. What remains will be pure. *(Let me burn in the fire, O Lord, so that what remains is of you.)* These are the days of tribulation. My vials are being poured out. I'm letting you know, my little children. Learn to stand in the storm. My presence is all around."

These are the days when we shall see the light of the Lord. Keep your eyes upon Him. We're going where we've never been before. Don't be afraid. This generation will see greater glory. *Be the flame. Burn, burn, burn as a fire.* Don't be afraid, my children. The land can be holy. Everything is crying holy! The land is crying holy!

I cried, "Come, LORD Jesus, come!! Save our children, save our families. Make every crooked way straight. One sound out of your Church – the cry of the heart! Come Lord Jesus, come! You want children who are not afraid, who say, 'Here am I.' Do not be afraid. The Lord is with us. Father, you will protect us.

Train us, Lord, to believe for the impossible! Open up every part of my heart! I want to change! I know you'll cover me. I will not be afraid. Let your light shine. Illuminate us, O Lord. Let the women be kindling, fire starters. Set the dead works on fire. The battle belongs to the Lord. Father, let the Deborahs arise. A company of women. Make us kindling that burns the dead works. A generation unafraid. Here am I! Anoint me, Lord. Anoint my hands and my feet. Send me forth! The bondservants, the pouring out of Your Spirit where the sons and the daughters prophesy."

Then the Lord spoke, "The books are open. The words are coming to life. Can you see it? Can you hear it? All things spoken, pouring out. The WORD is coming off the pages. The WORD is being poured out like liquid light. The WORDS are coming out of the Bible like liquid fire. Get immersed in the Holy Spirit, the River of God. Stay in it until it directs you – that is training ground. Be strong. People of the land be ready, for I am with you. That is what I covenant with you: I will shake all nations—the desire of the nations will come." I heard, "The Lord is pouring out. Your Word is being poured out. Jesus! Jesus!"

> *"It will come about after this That I will pour out My Spirit on all mankind; And your sons and daughters will prophesy, your old men will dream dreams, your young men will see visions...I will display wonders in the sky and on the earth, blood, fire and columns of smoke. The sun will be turned into darkness and the moon into blood before the great and awesome day of the Lord comes. And it will come about that whoever calls on the name of the Lord will be delivered" (Joel 2:28-32, NASB);*

"Father, thank you that you are going to make us salt, and repairers of the breach. We call upon Your Name, Lord. No agenda, only what You say. We call upon Your Name. Come, Lord Jesus, come! All the elect, the remnant, calls. Come, Lord Jesus, come. Manifest yourself!"

New Training Ground
December 26, 2009
The Lord began to teach us about the revival angel and how important it was to receive the angels of the Lord when He sends them. Daniel received Gabriel and began to walk in greater revelation of what was happening around him. We have learned when a city is under the dominion or influences of a principality, its people have the personality of that principality. When the Lord reveals the

revival angel over a city, you can move in the redemptive personality of the Lord for that city instead of the principality's personality. For example, the spirit over Charleston is pride. The revival angel over Charleston had a very humble spirit. The Lord wanted to redeem Charleston with humility. Heaven intends to destroy the works of the enemy, and the most effective way is to neutralize them. So, the Holy Spirit will come in the opposite spirit of that city.

December 31, 2009

I was battling discouragement, and I saw a bright ball of light. Jesus came out of the light toward me with hands open wide. I was on my knees before Him praying and crying out, "Lord, what is going on? Why am I having such horrible thoughts?" Then I saw in the spirit what looked like a big, black beetle in my right ear. It was huge, almost as big as I am. I prayed all day asking the Lord to remove it. He pulled it out and green liquid came out of my ear as it was removed. Finally, it was gone.

I believe the enemy planted the bug in my ear to speak doubt, unbelief, and discouragement. I had terrible thoughts of the fear of man, great fear, and what went in my ear came out my mouth. It took a day to defeat it. Seymour was attacked as well but was trying to combat what I was speaking. I finally started rebuking the devil. It was as Sally had said earlier—I needed to run.

January 1, 2010

As I prayed, I heard the Lord say in that sweet, quiet voice, "You are highly favored."

January 19, 2010

As I prayed, I saw myself kneeling at the feet of Jesus. His feet were a bronze color, and I could see the nail marks. He told me it is important to write all that I see, including the vision of the chariot I saw at Anson Street. I immediately got up from prayer and wrote it down. He said, "You will need many of them for a later time. The Holy Spirit will lead you and Seymour in many things you will do. Some things need to be remembered. The Day of the Lord is coming soon. My peace I give to you. Supernatural strength, walk in supernatural strength. I will give it to you."

January 29, 2010

I saw the Revival Angel at Anson Street. His robe was glistening white, as if it had tiny diamonds all over it. He held a stick that was about 20″ long. He was shaking the stick forward, and there was liquid (milk) on it. The milk splashed out as he shook it.

A huge bolt of lightning came from the ceiling straight down into the room about three to five feet in front of Seymour and me. It was about five feet wide and very tall. I said, "Lord, if what I am seeing is true, show it to me in your Word." I was going through Scripture and flipped the pages to Revelation 4. Verse five says, "Out from the Throne come flashes of lightning…" Within moments, a very shy young man who would not normally read in front of people, got up and read out of Ezekiel about lightning. The Lord gave me a double witness that this was HIM.

Suddenly, Seymour got up and began to run around in a circle exactly where the lightning had come down. The Lord told him to run around that area seven times. A Jewish brother got up and noticed what Seymour was doing and said, "You are doing what the Jewish bride does to the groom when he comes in. She walks around him seven times before they get married." The presence of the Lord began to fall each time something was said that was of Him. We began to have a greater sense of His presence. We were in awe at what the Lord was doing. When we were leaving, I saw the Angel of the Lord again. Something had been added to his outfit, it was a large medal-like gold broach or pin.

January 30, 2010

At Anson Street, I looked down at the bowl of prayer I carried in my being that the Angel of the Lord had given me. Blue and magenta incense were swirling, with rippling water beneath. Suddenly, numbers appeared on the surface of the water in the form of a clock. I thought I saw the hands at 11:50.

February 20, 2010

We had a move of God at our monthly ladies meeting as we followed the instructions of the Lord. He said, *"Call the people's spirits to attention. Don't minister soul to soul; minister spirit to spirit."* When teaching is done from soul to soul (with our head instead of our spirit), the teaching just rolls off of us like water off of a duck's back; but when the spirit man hears, the power of God manifests.

We obeyed and called our spirits to attention. The word (we are a royal priesthood with the power of God abiding within) was manifested in power to deliver. Some came to the meeting crying and depressed because of difficulties, but as the Word was being taught, the power of God fell and the spirit of depression left. Afterwards, one of the ladies was still not free. The Lord told me to call her spirit to attention and have her pray in the spirit. As she prayed, her countenance changed. The Lord said, "Now have her speak whatever she hears and have someone write it down." After hearing what was written down, she began to get free. It was awesome to see her soul go from depression to empowerment.

The women continued to pray for one another. Some moved in new giftings, others fell down under the power of God. During ministry, I saw myself standing on a high cliff with furry, newborn eaglets. I was encouraging them to step off the cliff and fly. As soon as the eaglets stepped off in faith, they turned into full grown eagles and began to fly. The sky was full of them. At first I thought they were going to bump into each other because there were so many, but they didn't. They formed into a unit and began to come into formation.

 Steps of Understanding
(Vision Interpretation):

The eaglets beginning to fly represented the women beginning to walk in their priesthood. They were being taught every point so they would have knowledge of how to follow in the spirit of God. As their spirit man came forth, they were illuminated from the inside out. Their whole being became light. One of the ladies saw a bucket of oil flowing in the center of where we were praying. She kept saying, "Get in the flow." We all stepped in. As we did, we were being anointed. The presence of the Lord moved in great power. We were on our faces before the Lord.

March 7, 2010

We were on our way to church for Sunday service, and Seymour was talking about the whirlwind of God. I looked out the front windshield of the car to our left, where I saw a thin column that looked like a whirlwind. I was going to tell Seymour to look at it, but as we passed by, it disappeared. I realized that I was seeing in the spirit so I asked the Lord to show me what was happening around us. I saw two angels dressed in white on either side of our car facing us as we drove down the road. They did not have wings. They were each holding a beautiful golden sword out in front of them. The tips of the swords were facing upward.

That afternoon in the service, it was as though Seymour and I were playing badminton with the Word of the Lord, taking turns speaking the Word of the Lord. It went on for about a half hour. The Lord was saying awesome things through us.

We need to ask the Lord what He wants to do with us and what He wants to say. There is so much glory the Father wants to give us. The Holy Spirit is so willing.

As I sat before the Lord and worshipped Him, I was carried before the Lord in the spirit. I saw the voice of the Lord like wind. It went forth in the form of a V. He was saying to all the earth, *"I am coming."* His voice had great authority and might as it went forth. We must learn to listen for His voice: *My sheep hear My voice, and I know them, and they follow Me (John 10:27, NASB);*

March 13, 2010

We were at a meeting where a friend was ministering on healing. Part of his ministry is to teach how the brain and body react when a person has unforgiveness, as well as the different diseases that come from that unforgiveness. As I led worship at this meeting, I saw the glory of the Lord rolling in from 50 miles out.

Later during the meeting, the minister had all of us forgive our fathers. I had already been through years of forgiving my step-father. I had forgiven him for many things. This time, I saw him as I prayed. I saw him as a young man of about sixteen years. The Lord was washing his hands and feet. Then I watched as my step-father was peeled away from head to toe and became a different age. He looked as if he were thirteen. The Lord kept washing him, pouring water over him. Then the peeling happened again, and he was seven; again and he was five or six. Finally, his arms were around Jesus' waist and his face was buried in Jesus. How glorious is that? The Lord loves to redeem us.

Near the end of the service, the minister had everyone come forward who wanted to do something for the Lord. Everyone in the place went and dropped to their knees before the Lord. He was talking about being around the Throne Room. He asked me to be prepared to sing. As I got up, I was in the Throne Room standing before the Lord. Fire came from the bottom of my feet and went up to my head. The fire of God began to consume me, and it became an outward manifestation. I began to shake from the core of my being, trembling at the presence of the Lord, and began to sing, "Holy, Holy, Holy." His glory filled the room, and the sense of His holiness was there all during worship. The songs the Lord had me choose for worship were about the glory of God.

As I was driving home afterwards, I asked the Lord about the angels around the throne that sing, "Holy, Holy is the Lord." Suddenly, I saw an angel. He was about three feet tall. The angel had a harp and was flying back and forth over the throne of God and singing, "Holy, Holy." This angel had two heads, with yellow hair ending just below his ears with soft curls. One head faced one way and the other faced the opposite way. I thought it strange, but then I remembered Ezekiel saw creatures with four heads.

When I told Seymour about it later, he said they were looking in the past and future and on the former and latter rain singing *Holy, Holy* over all. They were definitely saying something about the Alpha and Omega, the Beginning and the End. Concerning our God, all things are holy—past, present, and future!

March 14, 2010
Sunday afternoon I was getting ready for church. I was pondering the vision of the angel with the two heads flying back and forth over the throne. The thought came to me that there are other places in Heaven to visit. Because the thought just popped into my mind, I believe this was a "God thought." I had heard people talk about other places in Heaven, but I never thought to ask about going

to them. Then my carnal mind took over and I remembered someone talking about rooms that were filled with new worship. I thought I'd like to go to one of the worship rooms.

Within a few seconds of having those thoughts, instead of going to rooms of worship, I saw an old library with tall shelves. All the books were brown and old. I knew that it was a library about things past and future concerning the earth. I stood in one place in the middle of the library. I asked, "What book should I choose?" Suddenly, a big book appeared in the air before me. It was *The Book of Isaiah*. Then another book came forward, *The Book of the Dead*, then *The Book of Resurrection*, then a golden unnamed book, that opened up to me (in Hebraic fashion, from right to left) and out of it came a river that poured toward us.

Suddenly, The Lord spoke what this all meant. *The Book of Isaiah* was about what is coming alive in the land. In it, God is asking who will go for Him. It is about the ancient way being restored. Also, the Lord is proclaiming Himself to be God, and as God, He is fully in control of all things, and is setting all things in order. First, before you get up in arms about *The Book of the Dead*, you must understand that it was a book filled with things that God ordained that had living power within them. When He ordained the relationship with man to walk with him in the garden in complete fellowship and being taught by the Lord the mysteries of the Kingdom and of having dominion, this was a living, fluid relationship. When man fell, that relationship died, and was recorded in the *Book of the Dead*. When Jesus came and resurrected that living relationship, it came from the *Book of Resurrection*.

God resurrects things that have been lost. Everything God does is living joy, love, and peace are living attributes. We serve a living God. Nothing of Him is inanimate; rather everything is alive. Scripture says in the last days, the love of many will wax cold. That means that the love of many will die and lose the life that was in it. Love needs to be resurrected and turned into the golden work that God ordained it to be. Even ministry becomes a dead work that needs resurrection power to become the golden work that Heaven ordained.

The meanings of the four books are:

> ➢ The Book of Isaiah—Isaiah's prophetic word to Israel and the church. We are now seeing these words come to pass. (The hour we are living in is in the Book of Isaiah.)
>
> ➢ The Book of the Dead—Things that God ordained that were stolen from the Church through sin. (Man's religious spirit kills off the things of God.)
>
> ➢ The Book of Resurrection—God resurrecting those things that have been stolen from the church, a resurrected people walking in power. (This is when revival comes.)
>
> ➢ The Golden Book—The original design, the purposes of God. God's purposes made manifested in the earth. As it is in Heaven it is being revealed on earth. The secret things are being revealed—God, revealed to His people. (*PRAISE GOD! LET IT BE, LORD.* Down with religious dogma! Down with the ways of man!)

The Golden Book was the only book of the four that opened up to me (in Hebraic fashion, from right to left) and a river poured out of the book toward us. Later, I saw two other books come off the shelf. *Zechariah* came off first, and went in front of the first four books. Then *Zephaniah* went in front of *Zechariah* .

March 19, 2010

We were at Anson Street, and I saw the Angel of the Lord walk up to Seymour and me. His robe gleamed with a bright light. The light looked like a vibrating, iridescent rainbow of colors moving up and down his robe. Through the vibrating light of rainbow colors, the Lord was telling us that His promises are sure. We are learning the language of the Spirit. All of these visions are a language type. God is speaking to me through visions and I am learning how to interpret them.

March 23, 2010

I heard the earth in the United States begin to tear. Then, in a dream, I saw a flat map of the United States with all of the states represented. I specifically saw

California, Arizona, Ohio, Illinois, and Alabama and Louisiana) on fire. There could have been more states lit up but I don't remember.

March 27, 2010

On Saturday, I was in bed beginning to fall asleep when, suddenly, I was in the worship room in Heaven. I saw a golden harp and I discerned there were other instruments in the room. I knew they were in plain sight but I could not see them. I could only see the harp. It became small and I swallowed it. I knew the harp was inside of me. Sunday, I got up and led worship. It was different this morning. As I worshiped, I could see the harp playing inside me; I knew the vision I had on Saturday was true. One person commented that the worship had a sound of healing.

May 15, 2010

At our regular worship at Anson Street, I saw two huge angels who seemed to be 20′ tall. I was sitting on the stage facing the audience, and they were standing on either side of the room next to the wall. They had a red cord that was strung horizontally between them, with each angel holding an end. A beautiful, sheer white curtain hung from the red cord and was open at the center. It was a beautiful sight to behold. I knew this was an opening to something new from Jesus.

In front of the curtain was a golden metallic stone that glowed brightly and hung in midair. It was flat on top and rounded on the bottom. As I watched it, I noticed there were three Hebrew words written on the stone. I could only see the first letter. A Jewish friend was attending the meeting that night. When I described the letter to him, he told me it was Alef, the first letter of the Jewish alphabet. Someone else commented that it was the first letter in Psalms 119. The Jewish brother also said that in the Jewish Bible, the Alef will appear randomly. Scholars are not sure why, but it does. We believe Jesus was telling us He will be sending "suddenlies" to the church. I believe it will be a new thing.

May 22, 2010

We were at a meeting at a fellow minister's church. During worship, I could see everyone dressed in white robes with thin crowns on their heads. The robes were simple and had bell-shaped sleeves. The robes hung down just over their feet. Everyone that was born again had these robes. This is not the first time I have seen these robes on people so, at first, I did not pay much attention to them. But I noticed that just about everyone in the room had them on.

I could see jewels beginning to form around some of their sleeves. Some had jewels around the neck. I knew the jewels form around the sleeves of our robes when we reach for the things of the Kingdom in obedience to God. For example, they form when we choose to walk in forgiveness or when we walk in love. Some had one or two jewels beginning to form. They were like badges and were placed around the neckline as people turned their faces toward Him. Some had five jewels starting on the neck area; some had seven. Some people did not have any jewels on their garments. They had on simple, white garments and wore a crown. It was a glorious sight to see all God's people robed in their garments.

I noticed that those who had rank in the spirit or who had matured had on an outer cloak that hung down mid-calf over their white robe. Their outer cloaks were very beautiful with jewels covering many parts of them. There were rows of jewels on the sleeves and many jewels around the neck. Also, they had jewels that went down the front. These people wore a crown with a lot of jewels on them. The jewels were many colors. It was a beautiful sight.

We can sense those who walk in spiritual authority, those who have God all around them and those who have paid the price of obedience. They may not be honored in the natural, but God honors them in the spirit. They may seem like little nobodies, but Jesus honors them. I have seen intercessors who walk in great spiritual authority clothed in such beauty. Jesus has clothed them in robes of righteousness, and they had rank in Heaven. I've also seen people who are weak and feeble in their bodies but are mighty ambassadors of the King. They are humble in spirit and Jesus is all over them. We should not judge anyone by his or her outer appearance. Jesus has great treasures hidden in earthen vessels.

Later, we went out to dinner, and the Lord continued to show me people's spiritual clothing. I noticed young people walking past us who had on the blackest robes—blacker than black. It was an awful sight. I was seeing lost souls, and it was heartbreaking. I've seen witches wear black robes. That is what these young people's robes looked like, except their robes were darker than any earthly black. We need to get the sinners saved.

June 4, 2010

We were driving to Augusta to pick up a staff on which an artist had made beautiful carvings. As we were driving, I had a vision of a nuclear explosion. It was not wide like those on television; it was thin. I did not pay much attention to the vision until I saw it a second time. I knew the bomb went off in a city, but I was not sure what city. I prayed that the explosion would not come to pass.

June 5, 2010

I was in prayer and suddenly saw a beautiful tree. It was a large, golden tree with roots dripping golden oil, like golden fire. The tree was on fire and golden all at the same time. It was as though I were looking at a volcano in the form of a tree. It was beautiful.

June 11, 2010

While in prayer at Anson Street, I saw people that were burdened and carrying many worries about jobs, family situations, health problems. Then I saw them coming forward to let the Lord speak encouraging words through them. As each person spoke, I saw the old, worried person fall into ashes and a new person emerge. The new person was in the likeness of the old, but free.

The people at Anson Street began to pray and prophesy. As they were used by God, they were being encouraged. Jesus was speaking to them with their own voices. Then I saw a hand over my heart. The hand had a nail through it and was full of blood. I knew it was the hand of Jesus. I had been praying to see the full work of the cross in my life, and I knew I had received it. The full work of the cross was going to be a part of my heart.

In another vision, a butterfly began to come out of a cocoon, and I heard the word *metamorphosis*. I believe we were changed into something new. The worm has become a butterfly. We were gaining the strength to fly.

June 16, 2010

I was awake at 3:12 and felt I should stand before the Lord. I heard: *The Anointing of the Ages.* I was given a white staff and I held it in my hands. I could not sleep after that.

June 22, 2010

Seymour and I were at a prayer gathering with local pastors. Seymour started praying for Israel, specifically, Jerusalem. As he prayed, I saw a huge angel standing over Jerusalem. He opened his wings and spread them out over the city, forming a dome over Jerusalem. The Lord is bringing His light into a dark situation. I later found out that the missile system that protects Jerusalem is called the Iron Dome. A pillar of light came down over and between his wings. As I was seeing this, Seymour prayed that the angel's wings would cover the city. The vision and prayer were confirmation that the Lord is covering Jerusalem and keeping her.

June 25, 2010

At Anson Street, the song of the Lord was very sweet. Yet, the prophetic word from Zechariah had judgment all through it. The words were frightening; the scriptures were of judgment upon the land. In a vision, I saw the United States. Out of the Midwest, I saw a locust cloud. I heard and began to sing, *Rise,* and they rose from the ground like a dark cloud.

June 27, 2010

I was awakened by the word, *Legions.* When I heard the word, it frightened me. I knew that evil spirits would be released on the Church and on men and women, yet there was nothing we could do to stop it. My heart broke because I knew people were not listening to the many warnings and alarms that were going off. They were busy with their lives and their own ideas; therefore, they were not interested in God. Even church people would not make it a point to go to prayer meetings or to Anson Street, a place prepared by the Lord to train our spirit.

July 1, 2010

David Hogan, a missionary to Mexico, and their team of people trained in how to move with God in power have seen many people raised from the dead and had many other miracles occur in their ministry. He was speaking at our church today, he said that there would be a tsunami of demons released on the Church, carrying many away. Those that remained would be empowered.

Church! We must open our eyes and see what the Word and the Spirit is saying to the churches. This is as the days of Sodom and Gomorrah when people were busy with their self-centered lives and the angels came and destroyed the cities and towns.

July 3, 2010

I saw brother David Hogan and his team which included his two sons Jo-D and Luis. I looked further in the spirit, and I saw Debbie, David's wife, and she was covered for battle. Then I saw Cindi, Jo-D's wife, and she was also covered for battle. I knew God had trained them to be covered for battle. They were dressed from head to toe in silver. The covering had diamond-shaped chisels in it, especially around the front of the legs. It was somewhat like the covering on the character, C-3PO, from the movie, *Star Wars*. But it was one piece without openings at the joints, and it was flexible, not stiff. The metal was like taut fabric without wrinkles.

I saw David with the covering, and I could see that he had the freedom to move whichever way he was led to move. There was no part of his body exposed; I could not see his face or any body parts like his hands or feet. He was completely covered. It was a beautiful sight of a warrior clothed for battle, nothing seen but the redeeming power of God on a vessel used for His purposes. He also had a sword and a shield. David, his family, and his team were fierce in appearance.

July 6, 2010

I was in the Throne Room and I saw a bowl covered in a cloud. The cloud was blown away and I saw into the bowl, where there was clear liquid. Then I looked and saw someone signing a white piece of paper. I was seeing evil legislation being signed into law.

July 9, 2010

As I was praying, I went back to the place where I had seen the Fountain of Love with the angels, Faith and Hope, standing on either side of the fountain. I went into the fountain and washed myself and then sat down. I looked at Faith and he turned to me and said, "Train your words." I knew he was telling me to speak words filled with faith and not to speak doubt, unbelief, failure, or weakness.

Later, I saw people with a high Body Mass Index (BMI) being labeled as obese. They were fed a small amount of food. Those with a normal BMI were fed a regular amount of food. The Lord then led me to an article regarding the new mandate for obesity ratings for every American (the following is the exact mandate):

Obesity Rating for Every American Must Be Included in Stimulus-Mandated Electronic Health Records, Says HHS Thursday, July 15, 2010 by Matt Cover, Staff Writer.

Health and Human Services Secretary Kathleen Sebelius speaks to reporters at HHS headquarters in Washington on July 1, 2010. (CNSNews.com/Penny Starr)(CNSNews.com) – New federal regulations issued this week stipulate that the electronic health records--that all Americans are supposed to have by 2014 under the terms of the stimulus law that President Barack Obama signed last year--must record not only the traditional measures of height and weight, but also the Body Mass Index: a measure of obesity.

The obesity-rating regulation states that every American's electronic health record must: "Calculate body mass index. Automatically calculate and display body mass index (BMI) based on a patient's height and weight." The law also requires that these electronic health records be available--with appropriate security measures--on a national exchange. The new regulations are one of the first steps towards the government's goal of universal adoption of electronic health records (EHRs) by 2014, as outlined in the 2009 economic stimulus law. Specifically, the regulations issued on Tuesday by Health and Human Services Secretary Kathleen Sebelius and Dr. David Blumenthal, the National Coordinator for Health Information Technology, define the "meaningful use" of electronic records. Under the stimulus law, health care providers--including doctors and hospitals--must establish "meaningful use" of EHRs by 2014 in order to qualify for federal subsidies. After that, they will be subjected to penalties in the form of diminished Medicare and Medicaid payments for not establishing "meaningful use" of EHRs.

August 8, 2010

As I was preparing for Sunday service, I began to pray. A bright angel appeared to the right of me, glowing with the presence of the Lord. I prayed, "Lord, let this presence come through the veil to my realm. There is so much power on the other side of the veil where you are; let that power come over to my side."

Later, during worship, the presence of the Lord came with power. Through the speakers, I could hear other voices singing with me. I stopped singing and I could hardly hear their voices. As I started singing again, I could hear the voices singing with me. Many commented that God's presence came down in a powerful way as we worshipped. God does answer prayers.

That night in a dream, someone speaking in a Russian accent said, "We are in a state of emergency!" I awoke and wondered about the meaning of it since I had not watched the news in a few days. Some news programs were discussing the wheat shortage in Russia. Others were talking about fires around a nuclear plant. The following is an article written on August 10, 2010:

Moscow Resembles Apocalyptic Movie Scene

August 10, 2010 Russia Today
Experts have already called the current record-breaking heatwave the worst in a thousand years. With every other person wearing a mask, the city now looks like the center of a dangerous epidemic.....Rain is now as highly sought-after in Moscow as snow at Christmas....there is no imminent end in sight to these post-apocalyptic scenes.
http://rbth.ru/articles/2010/08/10/moscow_resembles_apocalyptic_mvie_scee 04870.html

September 5, 2010

We were at a church in Virginia. During praise and worship, I was praying and asking God to use us for His glory. Suddenly, in a vision, I saw the Throne of God. The throne was huge, and the arm rests were about four feet wide on either side. The whole throne had the appearance of solid, pure white marble. I was looking at it front and center. While in the Throne Room, I was praying for growth in our lives. I saw trees growing up on the left and right side of the armrests. The bark on the trees was white—it was part of the throne. The trees continued to grow almost equal to the back headrest of the throne. I could see silver dust sparkling all around the beautiful trees. (I was still praying about growth.) Then beautiful fruit appeared. The yellow and red fruit were perfect in appearance; they looked like Gala apples.

October 8, 2010

We were at Anson Street, and as we worshipped, I saw the Lord on a white horse. He had a white scroll in His hand with a gold trim around the edges. I asked the Lord to show me what was written on the scroll. Again, I saw in the spirit. This time I focused on the scroll. I saw three lines that became clear to me. The first said, "Hope for a future." The second line read, "The Kingdom come," and the third line read, "Resurrection." Then the gold trim lit up, glowing all around the edges.

I believe these words will be of great significance in our future and to the future of the church. God is giving His people hope for their future. It is not hope that the world gives, but it is life-changing and filled with peace. This hope is not in money, things, or man; but in the peace that God is in control. It is a resting hope.

The Kingdom is coming in a dynamic way. It is filled with the righteous—those doing what is right in the sight of the Lord, righteousness from God's view point. There is such joy when we do what is right and our consciences are clear. The Kingdom is also filled with peace; therefore, we must learn the way of peace and rest. We must quiet our busy minds and wills that are set against God. Walking in peace and rest keeps us from being anxious and overwhelmed by what we see and hear. We know that we cannot lose because the God of the universe is in control and everything submits to His will. Being at peace also helps us hear from God.

These things of the Kingdom bring us great joy, and we become like children, enjoying all the blessings of the Father. The pattern of the Kingdom is clear conscience, peace (no anxiety or worries), and enjoying what God is enjoying.

October 22, 2010

At Anson Street during worship, I knew something was different. I was singing about embracing the fire. I heard the Lord say, "Call up the oceans." I sang about the oceans and I called them up. Then three tall pillars of water appeared in the church. They had a twisted design in them, like towels being wrung out.

The pillars were in a row with the middle one slightly forward. The Lord later told me that when he appears, men walk in fear at His appearing. He said this was the case when He wanted to speak to Israel. I asked the Lord, "Could you take me to the verse?" I immediately went right to the verse, Exodus 19:16, which is about the Lord speaking to Israel from Mt. Sinai.

I stopped singing and began to discuss this chapter so we could find out what the Lord wanted to say in all this. The Lord was telling us not to fear when He comes, only believe. The third day has come and the Father is coming to His children and we need to receive Him and be prepared for His coming. After we ended our discussion, I said, *Jesus, come.* Jesus came and was gleaming white, standing in the middle of the three pillars of water. He stood there for a while, then turned and walked away. The three pillars followed Him. I knew He was telling us to follow Him in this way.

November 10, 2010

For days we had suffered great adversity. Our souls were in turmoil over various things about our ministry—the work of the Kingdom, and what the call was on our lives.

I was truly perplexed, so I told Seymour we needed to pray. As I lay before the Lord and began to pray, I saw a silver pitcher of the cleanest water flowing over my head. I could feel heat as the water flowed, cleansing my thoughts and emotions. I was wondering why the water was not flowing over and into my heart because I thought my heart needed to be clean. But I knew it was my head that needed to be washed of all the negative suggestions of the enemy. My spirit felt better, and I came to a place of peace and harmony with myself and God.

Chapter 16

Those Who Know Their God

December 31, 2010

We were resting before the Lord to pray in the New Year when I heard the Lord say, *"Great rest is coming to those who hear the Word. I am going to move the Heavens and the earth. People will run to and fro, but my people will stand strong for Me. Fear will prevail over many, but don't you walk in fear. You must have faith to make it through the days that are coming. Learn to trust."* Then the Lord gave me the meaning of rest. He said, *"Rest is trust—trusting that I will make the way even when you don't see anything, even when things seemingly are not changing."*

He said, *"Salvation will come to many souls that I am calling to the Kingdom. I am giving supernaturally to my sons and daughters. Goats on the left hand; sheep on the right. Don't be selective about what you hear from Me. Those that have let Me polish them are beginning to come forth."*

As I was writing these words down, I saw the glory trainers in the spirit. They train us for the glory by keeping us on track. As I was seeing them, I told the Lord, "I am ready to learn." I heard the Lord say, "Don't reject the things that are from above." Then I saw a whirlwind that was right-side up. Then it turned upside-down. It was white in color and looked like smoke.

I saw another door open in Heaven that led to a silver path. The path had white paver stones on each side. It was beautiful. Then I saw Jesus coming like a bright star in the sky. I heard the words, "money change." Then I heard, "Two will be given." I saw tanks moving across America.[6]

January 2, 2011

Seymour and I believe in training people to walk with God and to be used by Him. We do not believe that God meant for His house to be a "one man show." We are the Body of Christ, and each part needs to function just as each part of our physical bodies needs to function. If there are parts of our body that are not functioning, then our body is sick. The same thing is true of the body of believers. The Lord wants everyone activated; He doesn't need pew warmers. Everyone can do something in God, but it will only come to pass when we engage and work with the Holy Spirit.

Sunday, at church, the Spirit of God was moving. People were getting touched by the presence of the Lord. We had everyone praying for one another. Seymour and I moved out of the way so those that were praying could see it was their gift from God being used, and not ours. They were God's answer to that situation. While they prayed for each other, the gifts of God began to flow. People stood up and began to tell of visions they were seeing. Others heard words from the Lord. All the words confirmed what each person was seeing and hearing.

I then saw a pool of silver water. It was glistening as the light of His presence shined upon the pool. Then I saw that the people in the church had a silver bucket in each hand. They came up to the pool, dipped their buckets in the silver water, and walked away with a bucket that was full and overflowing. Each was rejoicing at what they had. I believe this is what was happening at our church. The silver is a picture of redemption. People's gifts were being redeemed, and the people were being used to redeem others. It was a beautiful sight.

---

[6] Note: *While my husband, Seymour, was searching the internet, he found an article which stated that as of January 7, 2011, the World Bank will be offering Chinese bonds. This is the beginning of the money change.*

January 7, 2011

I had a lot of questions to ask God. One of the questions was about Matthew 22:10-14:

> *Those slaves went out into the streets and gathered together all they found, both evil and good; and the wedding hall was filled with dinner guests. 11 "But when the king came in to look over the dinner guests, he saw a man there who was not dressed in wedding clothes, 12 and he said to him, 'Friend, how did you come in here without wedding clothes?' And the man was speechless. 13 Then the king said to the servants, 'Bind him hand and foot, and throw him into the outer darkness; in that place there will be weeping and gnashing of teeth.' 14 For many are called, but few are chosen" (NASB).*

The Hebrew meaning for friend in Verse 12 is comrade. A comrade is someone who is a colleague or an ally. There are two types of guests in this story, the good and the evil. The good believed God, And then there is the person who doesn't have on wedding clothes. The man not wearing wedding clothes is the one Jesus called friend. He worked for God but did not believe God. Working for God will not get you wedding clothes.

January 12, 2011

As I was praying, over and over again, I kept seeing tan tanks coming down the streets of a city. I did not know what state they were in or where they were. I prayed for the Lord to have mercy.

January 27, 2011

I saw people in a small room, huddled around what looked like a heater, which was turned on only when coins were inserted. They were paying for heat by using a coin operated heater that looked like a street parking meter, only bigger. It was 3' high by 24" wide. It did not heat a big area. I also saw a family dressed in gloves and coats. They were sitting around the heater to keep warm, but they had to keep putting coins into it for it to work. I prayed, "Lord, I hope we have wood for our fireplace."

Currently we have no breakdown of our national heating supply in America. As we know, our homes have central heating and are billed through a smart meter electronically.

This vision, however, revealed a time when rationed heat sources were limited to only one unit per home.

January 29, 2011

I was on my face before the Lord, repenting. I saw the feet of Jesus come up to my head. I put my hand out and grabbed His ankles. I saw other hands holding onto His ankles. Some of the hands were not hands of flesh but of hard material like clay or stone. It was as if a statue had grabbed hold of the Lord's feet. I saw a strong wind begin to blow at the Lord's feet. The hardened hands began to blow off of His ankles; they seemed to turn to powder and could not hold on. The fleshly hands held on with little effort, because they were living. These hands had the life of God in them.

I knew the fleshly hands represented those that had an intimate relationship with God—those that knew Him and heard from Him. The stone or clay hands represented those who had hardened their hearts. They had a form of godliness but did not know Him. When the Lord sent the wind, they were simply broken off like something hard and brittle, not having the strength to hold on to God.

> *"Not everyone who says to me, 'Lord, Lord,' will enter the Kingdom of Heaven, but only he who does the will of my Father who is in Heaven. Many will say to me on that day, 'Lord, Lord, did we not prophesy in your name, and in your name drive out demons and perform many miracles?' Then I will tell them plainly, 'I never knew you. Away from me, you evildoers!'"Therefore everyone who hears these words of mine and puts them into practice is like a wise man who built his house on the rock. The rain came down, the streams rose, and the winds blew and beat against that house; yet it did not fall, because it had its foundation on the rock. But everyone who hears these words of mine and does not put them into practice is like a foolish man who built his house on sand. The rain came down, the streams rose, and the winds blew and beat against that house, and it fell with a great crash" (Matt 7:21-27 NIV).*

February 7, 2011

As I was walking through my house praying, I saw horrible scenes of unrest in various places on earth. In quick succession, Kodak-like picture squares flashed rapidly before my eyes. I could not quite make out where these scenes were taking place, but I believe it was in the Middle East. There were fearful scenes of tanks and people rioting. I saw these scenes over and over again. Later I watched the news to see what was happening. Day after day a new nation began rioting. The news showed the whole top of Africa was fighting and rioting.

February 17, 2011

I awoke and I saw a vision of a clear, pure white ball being placed into Seymour's and my hands. The ball was as big as a basketball. Inside the ball, I saw miracles, signs, and wonders. The pure white ball was the move of God. I was holding it lightly in my hands and realized that moves of God come and go—we do not own them. They are given into the hands of leaders, and the leaders hold these moves lightly in their hands. That is why they so easily go away when the leaders' hands get stained with sin or with anything not of God. We must keep clean hands and pure hearts in order to hold onto the things God gives.

March 4, 2011

During our weekly Friday night prayer, I was taken to the White Throne and I was sitting at the feet of the Lord. I looked to the right of the throne room and it was as if a hole burned open in the wall. I was able to look down on the earth. Everything was black. I could see fire coming up out of the earth from what looked like two fissures. They were not covering the whole earth, just a mass of land. The fissures were very long and wide; it was as though two distinct lakes of fire were forming from each of the fissures. They seemed to go straight down two sides of the earth and then circle back in the center of both rivers of fire. I had the sense that earthquakes and volcanoes were causing these catastrophic events. I saw this vision three times. It was quite disturbing.

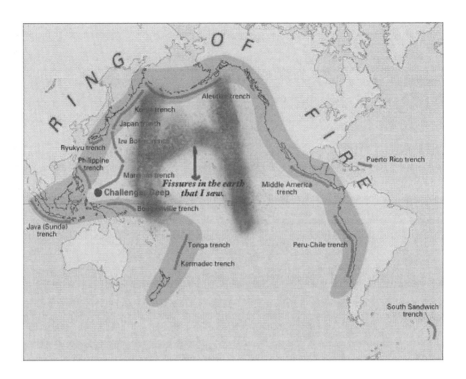

As we were praying, I saw rays of golden light covering me. Something was being deposited in my spirit. I began to write what I heard, "I am going to move in my power this year. I am going to put my house in order. My people will know it is Me. My power will gather and separate. Learn to be fire dwellers. Adversity will increase and with that increase, many will come into the Kingdom. Many will see My face and know Me on a personal level. Kingdom increase will be at the cost of many lives. I am planting a new foundation of those who will walk and talk with Me. Are you ready to run? Because I will not walk any longer. I am going to run in my power. Rise up, rise up oh warriors of the earth and hear the Word of the Lord. I am gathering! This is the time of the ingathering of the saints. Go, tell them my Words as a witness against them."

March 11, 2011
I was watching the news report on television about the earthquake in Japan. They were showing the nuclear plant. In a vision, I saw an explosion over the nuclear plant. Each time I watched the news report about the earthquake, I saw the same vision. I saw the vision three times that day. I wanted to call them and

tell them to get everyone away from that plant because I knew it was going to blow. On March 12, 2011 it blew up.

March 13, 2011

In a vision, I saw that those who loved and walked with God were falling away and becoming great God-haters. The reason they fell away was because they did not know His Ways. They had an idea of God, but it was wrong. They needed to humble themselves and repent. At the same time, those who humbled themselves under the mighty hand of God, walked greatly before Him. Humility is the way out of the great "falling away."

March 14, 2011

In a vision I saw a great wall of water. The first time I saw the tsunami it was being formed as it moved. I saw this vision throughout the day. That evening we were in a meeting with a couple from our church. As they were talking, I saw the water go out. I thought that maybe the water was going away. Right after that, I saw a tower of water coming up like a huge wave. I was very tiny compared to the height of the wave of water. I thought I might be seeing a spiritual tsunami instead of a natural tsunami. That night I felt led to watch the news. They were saying that the coast off of California was full of fault lines and that if there were a volcanic eruption from those fault lines, the resulting tsunami would cause a 100 ft. wave to come at California with such force that it would travel farther inland than the one that hit Japan.

Massive Earthquake Hits Japan

An 8.9-magnitude earthquake hit off the east coast of Japan early today. The quake—one of the largest in recorded history—triggered a 23-foot tsunami that battered Japan's coast, killing hundreds and sweeping away cars, homes, buildings, and boats. (*Editor's note: we'll post more as the story develops -- Lloyd Young*)

They said this was going to happen because several earthquakes and volcanoes had already hit various locations in the Ring of Fire (see illustration above), and the earth land mass was moving and that California was coming next.

I believe what the Lord showed in the vision He gave me on March 4, 2011 of the two rivers was that there would be two major earthquakes that would happen in the earth. The first was Japan and the next one was California. I awoke the next morning and thought about when the Lord told me to *"Cry 'mercy', for the whirling wheels have started to turn."* I thought maybe God wanted me to stand in the gap and pray so that some things would not come to pass. I began to cry mercy over the next quake and I saw the rivers immediately close up.

I pray that this does not happen in California. It would truly wipe out California as well as other places. The evil in California is so great. I wish the people would have a revival and repentance would come to them. Our land is evil and there needs to be a cry for God to come and fill empty souls. I believe God wants to move upon all people so they can see their state so that they would cry out to God to move upon them.

March 18, 2011

I was sitting at the Pastor's Table, a monthly meeting of local pastors. The pastors were discussing walking in love. I went into an open vision. I was standing outside looking up at the sky. There were thick clouds. The clouds were turning counter clockwise. As the clouds turned, they were forming a whirlwind. The color of the clouds were red and white. After the tsunami in Japan, there was a huge whirlwind or swirling vortex in the water. That is what it looked like only it was in the sky, and it was white and red.

April 17, 2011

It was Sunday morning and we had a week of being busy with visitors. We had a couple in from China. They ministered at our home group. The next morning I was really carrying a burden and was crying out to God to come and deliver the people. He needed to come in His power. There are so many that need to be set free from the weights and chains that bind them.

I cried and cried for the people. I repented of all I had done. I was at the Throne of God and my head lay at His feet. A scroll of parchment appeared in the air to my right. It opened up and the word "HOPE" was in the center of the page. I watched as it turned into a living person and walked off the page and stood beside me. Another parchment scroll appeared. It opened, and the word

"BELIEVE" was on it. The word turned into a living person and came and stood beside me. The next scroll was "FAITH." Again, the word turned into a living person. On the last scroll was the word "LOVE." This time the word turned into a whirlwind and came and stood beside me.

I knew these living words would walk with me. I saw a white light, then I saw white pearls raining down on me. They fell out of nowhere. As I thought about the light, it would turn different colors, like a rainbow, then go back to white light. I believe these pearls were revelations from God and that as I thought and really looked at the revelation God was giving, the revelation would begin to have a deeper spectrum of understanding, just as light has a multi-dimensional spectrum. He was giving me greater wisdom and understanding of His ways and the revelation would always be pure, which is why the color turned back to white.

April 29, 2011

I was crying out to God as I prayed, and I heard the whisper: *Not long now.* Then I was handed a scroll with ornate golden ends. I opened the scroll and the word HOPE was written on it, filling the page. Later, I prayed alongside Seymour and I saw a garden with a huge, white waterfall. The waterfall cascaded down the middle of the garden. I knew it was time for me to wash myself again—wash away the world with its discouragement and negativity. I really needed to wash and receive joy and peace.

Two days before, we were praying during home group and the Lord took me to another garden He had taken me to many times before. He said, "You must learn to walk in peace. Rest here so that you might be trained to have peace." It was easy to look at life's circumstances, get overwhelmed, lose focus, and walk in fear, worry, and dread. The garden was His Garden of Peace. It was a very beautiful, green valley with grass that was alive.

July 18, 2011

While in prayer I saw the library again that held the books that were of this earthly realm. Another book came off the shelf. It was the book of Ezekiel. As I prayed further, I saw a bucket of light being poured out. The light was never ending—the pouring was continuous.

July 19,2011

As I awoke, I knew I had a dream that was from the Lord. I had dreamed the same dream twice. I was sitting in a chair and an orange colored smoke swirled around me, creating a whirlwind. It was a thin whirlwind of orange smoke, maybe five inches in length. As it swirled over me I heard, "Keep on seeking me." This happened twice in the same dream. That night, I was praying for the state of the church. I was handed a gold plate. Later I prayed, "Lord, help us to give life to this dying church." I saw myself by the River of Life. I reached down with one hand and scooped up a handful of water and drank from the River. Then I cupped both hands and scooped up a lot more. It was refreshing to my soul, and I was so blessed by God's presence. As I continued to pray, I saw waves of water overtake the borders of various southern cities. I believe they could have been tsunamis; walls of water rushing in on the land. Later in bed, I saw a white cloud forming a small whirling wind that hovered over Seymour and me. I thought, *What is this cloud?* In response, I heard, *"It is Lord Holy Spirit."* After this, I began to see it many times hovering over us.

July 23, 2011

God's amazing grace does what we cannot do. Humanity and the Church have walked away from grace because we think that we have all the answers. We think we know it all. However, it is God's amazing grace that causes everything to happen. Even the wisdom of the wise is futile compared to the one that walks in the Grace of God. Grace is the power to do what God called us to do from our birth.

The moment we think it is us and our call to do, we have fallen from grace, and we muddle things up until we once again realize that it is only God's amazing grace that does all things. Sometimes we accomplish much, or bring numerous souls into the Kingdom. But God says, *"I did that."* It is not by the preacher's words or by his works or by his efforts; it is by the grace of God.

August 11, 2011

I was leading praise and worship at church and stepped into the spirit realm. I saw a golden, narrow path. It looked like thousands of golden nuggets. You needed golden shoes to walk on this path. I was in the middle of it; I had on golden shoes. Then I was off the path with black shoes. Then I was on the path with golden shoes. This went back and forth then finally I stayed on the path.

Steps of Understanding
(Interpretation):

The golden nuggets were all the insights the Lord was showing me. I needed faith and a believing spirit to walk this path. I also needed to stay pure and holy before Him. I would get caught up with people and doing the business of church, and I was off the path. I also would get caught in the trap of doubt and unbelief. I would not write down some of my visions as the Lord spoke to me to do; I would forget or think it was not important, but then I would see the things the Lord spoke would come to pass and their significance. I needed to learn to stay on the path of Holy glory and not stray off. I was also learning obedience and humility.

Chapter 17

Taking the Gates

August 17, 2011

We were in prayer about the gate of our city. Seymour had done a lot of research and found the gate of Charleston, SC. We knew the Lord wanted us to pray at the gate of the city. The Lord first told us to see the mayor and ask him an important question: *"When I [God] move in this city, will My move be a blessing or curse for your plans for this city?"*

We met with the mayor and asked the question. Since we had already been told it was not important that we know the answer, we told the mayor, "It is not important that we know your answer." The mayor asked us what this "move" would look like. Seymour told him of other revivals in other cities and he replied, "A blessing, of course." He was polite to us, and we left. The Lord told Seymour to go to other places of government to ask permission to pray at the gate. We did, and the Lord opened wide the gates of the city.

The Lord led us to go on the 17th of August to worship Him as the Audience of ONE at the gate of Charleston. The forecast was for heavy showers and wind, but the Lord calmed the weather. We had about 40 people gather at the gate where we all worshiped the Lord. I saw a whirling wind appear over us. We were in awe to realize the Lord would hover over that spot. What we did not know was when we left, God the Father would stay. You can go this day to that gate and simply bow—and God the Father will meet you there, in His glory.

August 29, 2011

We went to Chicago for a conference. It was put on by a ministry that was out of Africa. This ministry was hosting a conference for people from all over America and the world. It was an awesome experience. On the third night there, I heard the Lord say, *"Go on a non-talking fast."* I thought, *Isn't that something that nuns and monks do?* I quickly dismissed the thought and went on to sleep. I never spoke a word to Seymour or anyone about what I had heard, because I thought it was a strange thing to think.

The next morning we were down for breakfast with two women we had met the night before. Seymour jumped up suddenly and said, "I've got to go write down what I heard about the "Silence of God." I was shocked—I immediately remembered what I heard the Lord speak the night prior. Then the lady we were sitting with said she knew of a young 18-year old woman who recently was told by the Lord to go on a non-talking fast. She stated that it was something nuns and monks practiced. At that moment, I knew God had spoken to me and that this was important.

Years later, we understood what the Lord was speaking to us. The leaders of this ministry were breaking fellowship and splitting at that conference, and it would be the last time we would be together with them as a team. Many things have happened in this ministry since we heard this word. The Father loves for us is to be in unity, and fellowship was broken. There is nothing for the Lord to speak to those in broken fellowship, but go and make it right with your brethren.

God was speaking to us about future events that were to come. He spoke to me about the Courtroom of Heaven. I kept hearing the word "release." It had to do with moving with the Spirit of God. He was talking to me about having an offense, that if we refuse to release the offense from our heart before the Lord, that "case" goes into the courts of heaven. It goes before the throne where only truth can stand. All things are laid open and bare before Him.

And when He had said this, He breathed on them and said to them, "Receive the Holy Spirit. If you forgive the sins of any, their sins have been forgiven them; if you retain the sins of any, they have been retained" (John 20:22-24).

I remembered my vision of standing before the throne as a tall dark angel was accusing me. Jesus is our defender, praying that we will forgive as He forgave us. The enemy is the prosecutor, accusing us that we have not obeyed the pattern the Father laid out through His Son. The Father is the Great Judge over the matter. Then there are the litigants, the offended and the offender(s). I understood that when our lives are caught up in the courts of heaven and there is a case before the throne, there is no work of Heaven this person can do. They are stuck, and the enemy is allowed to vex them and attack them until they do it God's way. Better to settle conflicts quickly so that we can get on with the true work of the Kingdom.

This word answered so many questions I had placed before the Lord; why He would tell me to minister to people in a myriad of ways for forgiveness. He has been trying to get his forces out of the courts and moving with Him!

But one whom you forgive anything, I forgive also; for indeed what I have forgiven, if I have forgiven anything, I did it for your sakes in the presence of Christ, so that no advantage would be taken of us by Satan, for we are not ignorant of his schemes (2 Cor 2:10-11).

We arrived home after the conference to host Jo-D and Cindi Hogan, missionaries to Mexico who worked with their father David Hogan. We were busy with them and on the third day of their visit, I completely lost my voice. We knew we were to start the fast August 29th of 2011. I had told one of the ladies that worked in the office. She asked, "How can you possibly do that?"

I came in on Sunday, and she was surprised to hear me talk about another confirmation as we drew close to the date of the fast. I needed these confirmations, otherwise I would have quit. This type of fast is very hard, and takes much discipline. You must concentrate very diligently. Talking is automatic—you think, and then you speak unconsciously. If you focus on thoughts, you will speak before you know it. I did this a couple of times. The morning of the second day, I immediately woke up in a vision. I saw the heavens open and there was gold pouring down like lava flowing over us. I guess the Lord was saying *"Keep going, be obedient even when you don't understand."*

September 25, 2011

I awoke meditating on the gospels, Pentecost, Paul's life, and the life of the first church. I pondered how angels interacted with them; how an angel told Philip to talk to the Ethiopian, and many others who saw angels.

My heart was broken because so many times I have had an unbelieving spirit, often because of others who have sown doubt and disbelief into my spirit. I began to weep before the Lord, asking for forgiveness. I longed to go back to Anson Street as it was a safe place for me. God's presence was there with power. At that moment the Lord opened my eyes. He showed me all the angel helpers he had sent—they were all there. I saw the Revival Angel—he was there as well. The bowl the Lord had given was still there. God is so merciful; even when we hesitate and listen to the doubt and unbelief of others, He never takes back what He has given us. I felt forgiven and loved by my Father. I began to weep all the more because of His kindness toward me.

Pondering Anson Street, I remembered that Seymour saw two large angels at the back door beckoning us to go out. I then knew that the Lord had finished with us there, and nothing I had done or thought caused it to end. Many times I felt maybe we were wasting our time because few people showed up, and they did not believe me when I said I saw the Revival Angel of Charleston. I, too, began to doubt even though I saw many convincing proofs that he had shown me these things. My faith began to weaken, and I would question why we were there; what the purpose of our presence was. I thought that somehow because I did not believe, I opened the door to the enemy to attack us and throw us out.

But no one can open or close a door except God. God needed us to go out to do battle elsewhere, similar to what He did with the early Church, allowing persecution so the Church's message could spread abroad. I am sure they longed for that time of fellowship and miracles when the Holy Spirit fell. When we grow, like baby eagles, God pushes us out of the nest so that we can learn to fly.

December 14, 2011

We were at home group in a circle praying. I saw a pathway in the darkness. This pathway went upwards toward the Lord. The path was very straight and narrow. It was a silver and blue color. These colors mean communion, revelation and redemption. Overhead was a whirling wind. Seymour and I, as well as those who followed us, were walking on the path. Later we prayed again and I saw a white chariot go over our heads. It was being pulled by white horses, and it was being driven by someone. There was gold writing on the chariot and on the wheels; all the trim was gold.

> *If you have run with footmen and they have tired you out, then how can you compete with horses (Jer 12:5)?*

December 20, 2011

In prayer, I saw the circumference of the earth. It was very dark. I was standing in South Carolina looking at the east coast, and somehow Seymour and I were standing on the earth—we were very large. Then I saw one golden spear fall to earth. This spear had rings of jewels around the top part, and went about 12 inches down. The jewels were crystal clear, and there were two rows of them. After the first spear fell, I heard and saw four more spears falling to the earth in various places along the east coast. We had been seeking the Lord for an east coast revival.

After the Lord had showed me the spears being thrown down to the earth, Seymour and I began to pray for the Lord to show us where else He would move in the earth. The Lord began to show Seymour the cities as we prayed and sought Him.

January 13, 2012

The Lord led us to go and find the gate keepers of Washington, DC and the surrounding areas (such as Virginia and Maryland). We went to a very good friend of ours who pastored a church in the Virginia area. Seymour asked him if he knew of people that were praying at the gates of Washington, DC.

It so happened that there was a couple that had just started using their church. They had been praying in Washington for years and had just moved into our friend's church to conduct continual prayer vigils. He told us about them but they would not be available to see us until the week of the 9th. We returned that week and God opened the door for us to see many of the gate keepers in various counties in Virginia and Washington. They were all coming together for the express purpose of prayer and seeking the face of God through the vehicle of praise and worship to the Lord. I saw these places as fire pots set in different localities throughout the city of Virginia and Washington.

On January 13, we went to a prayer meeting in Washington called Gate Post DC. It was a group of young hearts praying at the gate. The group had been there for many years, led by an intercessor and her children. A young man was to take over the work and this night he was being set in. The Lord ordered the steps of a brother who had raised up a house of prayer in Israel and had been there for seven years. He had to stay in the states for two additional weeks, so he stayed and we were there at this very special beginning.

We were amazed as we watched God put all the pieces together for the building of His gates of His city. As the group worshiped, I saw two swatches of incense that looked like brush strokes that hung in midair over the worship team. They were about two feet wide by four feet tall. One brush stroke on the left was blue, it was high over the worship team. The other brush stroke was magenta, it was on the right and hung a little lower. There were two angels in between these two strokes of incense.

We sat on the left side of the room. The speakers were ahead of us and on our right. An angel came out and stood to the left of the speaker and I saw him. He had a blue banner that went across his chest, right shoulder to left hip. He had white hair (a servant of the Ancient of Days anointing). He said he was the Revival Angel of Washington, and he handed me a key made of pure gold. It was ten inches long (government of GOD). It was a big key. He said, *Set things into order. Keep seeking the gatekeepers. Shout freedom at this gate. Set the rings in order* (all the groups, and how they relate). He handed me a spear and then after a while as I watched him, a crown appeared on my head. He stayed a while as I watched him, and the banner began to have a lot of little lights that began to glow (these are other anointed vessels, light bearers, from Washington and beyond who come to the Washington move of God. These lights reminded me of little stars. He stayed a little while longer and then left.

As soon as I came out of the vision I began to ask the Lord to give me a confirmation of it. The moment I spoke this, the speaker began to talk about the kingly anointing (the crown I saw). He said the church is moving from the priestly anointing which is worship, to the kingly anointing which is proclaiming the word of the Lord. This was my first confirmation. The next day we were to go to breakfast with a couple that we knew in Virginia.

We met at a place where neither of us knew that the speaker the night before would also be meeting. They were at a different table, but we were introduced to them by our friends who were hosting them for breakfast. As we sat at the table with the couple, the Lord spoke to me to tell them what the Lord showed me the night before. They said after hearing the vision, that there was a prophecy spoken years ago about someone with a key from Charleston who would come and bring revival to their area. This was my second confirmation. Then, as we were leaving, the minister from the night before spoke to Seymour and me, asking if they could give us a word from the Lord. They said we would "pick up anointings we did not earn, and that the Lord was giving us a spear." I thought, *Wow, I asked for a confirmation, and out of the mouths of strangers the Lord spoke His words again to me.* I knew that if I did not believe in such convincing words, I was an unbeliever. I chose to believe God and wait on the manifestation of His words.

January 19, 2012

I had been praying in the spirit for many days. I was doing it unconsciously. I awoke the morning of the 19th after having been in prayer most of the night. Every time I awoke I was in prayer. As I got up, I prayed and saw, as it were, a fiery whirlwind coming out of my mouth going up to Heaven. It was awesome; as I prayed it went up before the Lord. Later that day I got a text from a friend who said that the glory of the Lord would fall because of the prayers of God's people. That was a confirmation I was seeing what the Lord showed me.

February 7, 2012

I felt led to go on Facebook. Someone had posted a video of a well-known evangelist from Africa. I stopped what I was doing and began to listen to his message which was about repentance; the speaker carried an anointing for calling people to repentance. As I listened to his powerful words, I began to examine myself for anything that was not pleasing in the sight of the Lord. The speaker spoke of our ways, how we go about our day to day lives and that God is there, observing our ways.

I cried out to the Lord, "Lord, I love you more than Seymour, my children, even my grandchild!" I said, "Lord, I love you." I continued to cry out to Him. Suddenly, the presence of God came upon me. It was fearful. I felt as if I were in great agony. There was no place I could get comfortable—the weight of His presence was so heavy that I felt like I was having a heart attack. The heaviness on my chest was like a round disk right in the center of my chest that got heavier and heavier. I became frightened. I cried, "Lord, I will not give up! Have your way with me, oh Lord!"

I lay on my side on the floor. I was pinned there, and could not move. As I continued to pray, I could feel heat on one side of my brain, and then the heat went to the back of my brain. I heard: *And a leper came to Him and bowed down before Him, and said, "Lord, if You are willing, You can make me clean" (Matt 8:2).* I cried out all the more, and then I heard: *For the law of the Spirit of life in Christ Jesus has set you free from the law of sin and of death (Rom 8:2).*

The weight was so heavy. I began to see that if this came upon people, and they were resistant to God, how they would curse God as it is shown in the scriptures of Revelation. I began to cry out for Jesus to help me. I cried over and over again, *Jesus, help me, help me!* I was determined to endure whatever I was going through. I kept hearing the words "from death unto life." I heard this phrase repeatedly. I had a picture of Jesus in the garden praying when blood began to flow from His temples. I expected Seymour to tell me I was sweating blood. My mouth became very dry. I must have cried out all the water in my body. After a while, I heard the Lord say, "Go to bed and rest."

I went to bed, shivering, my body chilled from the whole experience. I turned on the Word and listened as I slept. At the time I was utterly drained and could not begin to process what had taken place, but I believe it was intercessory prayer for the Body of Christ to be purged from all its ungodly ways—the way the Church thinks and sees. The Lord wants to remove coldness of heart, and to restore the dry places in His house. He wants to press out all the sin that needs to be laid down on His altar. Because I was experiencing this, I was more than willing to give it all to Him. The next day, I could not talk or function. All I could do was sit still and be quiet before Him.

The following week we went to a meeting. I saw other intercessors who were in prayer, and they were going through the same experience that I had several nights before. I knew the Lord would do a deep cleansing in His house of all things not like Him.

February 9, 2012

We went down to Washington Square in Charleston where they have a lot of Masonic symbols. We had gone there earlier in the year before we had prayed at the gate. That time, as we stepped into the square it was as if we were walking into a room, even though we were outside in the open air. On the walls of this room were gargoyles that moved along the wall as we walked past. They were watching us intently.

This particular day we were returning to the square to show a few people some of the interesting things the Lord had shown Seymour concerning it. As we approached the square this time, I saw a bright light emanating from both Seymour and I. The light went out from us about 20 feet. I saw the gargoyles again, but this time they backed away from the entrance of the gate to the square. They did not want the light to touch them. I got so excited about the scene I was seeing, but heard the Lord say, *Do not rejoice at this, but rather rejoice that your name is written in the Lamb's book of Life.*

He said these words several times to me. I had to settle my spirit and align it with His. I became very sober in my spirit and realized the Lord did not rejoice over these fallen spirits that were not able to come into the joys of His glorious light. This was a deeper training ground for Seymour and me. We were learning how the Lord views a thing, and that we had to adjust our ways.

February 10, 2012

As I prayed, I saw people on two sides of a line. I saw two men standing on one side dressed in black rags. On the other side I saw three men in white. One, who had blonde hair, held a helmet with wings on it under his arm. The men on the dark side (on the left) and the men on the right side faced each other.

Steps of Understanding
(Interpretation):

I believe this is a vision of two types of people in the Lord's house. One group is covered in sin, and they are wearing rags. They have not cleansed themselves, and they have no spiritual fruit. The other three men represent those filled with the Spirit of God (Father, Son and Lord Holy Spirit). They are dressed in white, and some have grown to the point that their thoughts are higher than this old world. They are thinking the Lord's thoughts. The thoughts of God are the source of their strength (helmet under his arm: *He has done mighty deeds with His arm; He has scattered those who were proud in the thoughts of their heart (Luke 1:51).* They are being led by the Lord. They hear and obey only Him!

Chapter 18

BELIEVE!

The Black Cane

March 3, 2012

We started our day going to a solemn assembly of people praying over Washington DC at an Ethiopian church in downtown Washington. There were people there from all over Virginia and Washington. They were there preparing for the prayer gathering that minister Lou Engle would head up in March.

The Lord spoke to us days earlier to go to the Washington Monument and strike our rods three times to the ground. Several days before we were to go, I was questioning whether or not I really heard the Lord speak these words to me. Upon thinking this, I would see the Angel of the Lord over Washington pointing, saying to go. He was pointing toward the place we were to go, with a countenance unwavering and sure. I knew in order to move into the things of Washington, D.C. we could not be timid or unsure; we needed to decide and not move from that position. I saw this picture several times. So we wanted to be obedient to the call of the Lord. I knew that if I was imagining these things, we were going to be in trouble. The things we were about to do were very serious, and should not be undertaken lightly. So I asked the Lord for one more sign.

I had read a book called "The Harbinger" and it was filled with prophetic signs, or harbingers. I asked the Lord to give me a harbinger for our assignment in Washington. As we approached the site where we were to strike the ground, an elderly man came up to us. He had pure white hair and was wearing a light blue checkered shirt and tan slacks. He was carrying a black cane with a gold handle on top. I looked into his face and smiled. I thought to myself: *This is my Harbinger*.

Seymour and I both saw this man, and we both looked directly at him. He stood about five feet away from me. Days later, we both described what we saw. Seymour saw a younger man around 40. He had black hair and was carrying the same black cane. We realized we each saw two different people. At that point we acknowledged he was an angel sent from the Lord to strengthen our faith. We were sent to that spot of ground to proclaim these words: "In the name of Jesus, I declare the "*Spirit of Judgment, the Spirit of Justice, and the Spirit of Freedom!*" The Lord told Seymour, *"In the name of the Lord Jesus Christ of Nazareth and of Heaven, I release the Spirit of Justice and the Spirit of Righteousness upon the land from here in Jesus' name."*

Seymour and I began to talk about what had happened after we struck the ground. As we were talking, Seymour felt the power of God. Seymour believed the ground was taken, and awaiting someone bold enough to go sit in a chair and bask in the presence of the Lord, awaiting the Lord's moment for the city. I saw in the spirit that when we struck the ground, there would be concentric circles that would go out from our rods, like ripples in a pond.

March 10, 2012

I awoke this morning feeling bad, like some kind of oppressive spirit was against me. I began to talk to Seymour and He said, "Do you want to give up? We can't give up." I could hear myself talking, and it was as if my flesh was going on and on. I knew then that I had to die from my ways, my will, and wants. So I did so in prayer, and at that moment I could see these white horses that were running very fast. I had seen them days earlier, and their feet were pawing at the ground like they wanted to get moving. I was glad they were running. That meant that something was about to explode, and I was ready for any movement of the Spirit of God. Our ladies were meeting later that day, and the theme that year was prayer. We would choose a theme every year and walk in that theme, until what we were learning lived in us. As we got in a circle to pray, I saw angels all around us. Their wings were pointed upward toward Heaven. I saw a round metal cylinder that was full of light, and it hung in midair. I reached out and grabbed it. I had seen these cylinders several times, and each time, I would reach and grab it. I am not sure why I keep seeing the same things over and over again.

March 15, 2012

3:38 am: I was awakened out of sleep; I was very tired. Jesus came and took my hand said, *I have a very important job, and I need you to do it*. He told me to get up and write this down: *The hour is late.*

March 18, 2012

I was awakened with the Lord speaking to me a name: Obed. Then I heard it again, but different. Obed-Edom. As I fell back to sleep, I thought to myself, *I will remember that name.* I awoke a second time and thought the name was Leo. Then I heard again Obed, then again, Obed-Edom. I told Seymour when I arose what I had heard, and knew we had to look up what it all meant. We found that it was a man whose home was where the Ark of the Covenant of the Lord was placed after a tragic incident of disobedience caused the death of one of the Israelites carrying the ark. David paid a heavy price to learn the importance of carrying the ark back to Jerusalem properly. Yet, while the ark was at Obed's home, everything he had was blessed. We knew this story was saying we were to keep the Ark of God's presence, and that presence was to be preceded by intimate worship. That is how David was to carry the Ark of the Covenant.

March 24, 2012

As Seymour and I laid before the Lord I saw an angel standing at my right side. He was fully engulfed in flames and the flames were flickering in the wind. He reached down and put his hand on our hearts and there appeared fire pots in our hearts. Our hearts were set on fire for the Lord to a greater degree. Thank you Lord, for setting our hearts ablaze for you!

March 25, 2012

We would often listen to the Word as we slept. We did this so that our subconscious minds would hear the word of God as we slept. This particular day as I was listening, as I awoke I heard the narrator of the beginning of the book of Revelation say that this book was written masterfully. I thought to myself as I heard this, *Lord, I wish I had the ability to write things that way.* I thought myself to be a horrible writer. I was good at other things, but writing was not one of my strengths.

As I said this to myself, I saw a man come up to me. He had eyes all over his face and everywhere else on his body. Jesus was standing to his right. I said to myself, *I receive this vision. I will not turn away from it nor deny that I am seeing what is before my eyes.* I looked at him and said, "I choose to believe." At that very moment, the word of God that was being read spoke these words. "He had eyes of fire." The word "eyes" was accentuated. So I knew the vision that stood in my minds eyes was real. Next, I heard, "I saw four living creatures with four wings and they were covered in eyes." Again, the word "eyes" stood out to me as the scripture was being read. Now I had seen all four living creatures. Sunday we went to church. The Lord had been showing me that when we are faced with the Spirit of God and see from God's perspective, our natural man starts to war against the things of the spirit.

> But the natural man receiveth not the things of the Spirit of God: for they are foolishness unto him: neither can he know them, because they are spiritually discerned. 15 But he that is spiritual judgeth all things, yet he himself is judged of no man (1 Cor 2:14-15).

That is why I was filled with doubt and unbelief. I was amazed at the lack of faith I had in God. I thought I had faith until I began to experience these things. My natural man would fight God with the hurt and the woundedness I had received in my youth.

I realized I was filled with rejection and failure. I also saw that I had been discipled by the enemy. He had trained me, teaching me that I was not good enough. In order to move forward instead of circling back around in different situations, I needed to unlearn this old program and respond on a different level of faith. I needed to have God's level of faith and not my own natural faith.

I saw that Heaven was willing to give me everything it had. All of what Heaven is and all it contains was made for me. This was too good to be true. Yet I saw Jesus willing to give me precious things that were His. He gave them to me with no strings attached. They were mine to have. Not because I was special or had done anything for them. He gave them to me because He loved me. I would hear these words, "Fear not little flock, it is the Father's good pleasure to give you the kingdom.

As we went to church that afternoon, the service was powerful. I shared with everyone how to recognize your spirit man from your natural man. I began to recognize that when the Spirit of God comes, immediately your natural man goes to war against you. The natural man will try to put an end to us being used by God. God will say to your spirit man, "Go and lay before me in front of everyone, wave a banner, raise your hands, go and tell someone a word of encouragement,"etc.. The natural man will hear the command, then protest and reason why we should not do what we heard. All of the arguments are quite logical and practical. God does not ask us to be logical or practical. He simply says, "Obey me." *My sheep hear My voice, and I know them, and they follow Me.*

Many lives would be changed if our spirit man would follow God and obey Him. The Church would be different. I spoke of this that Sunday and many put to death that opposing voice within to follow their spirit man. Jesus was glorified in His church and His children learned to be discipled by the Spirit of God (*John 10:27*).

April 8, 2012

I saw a flaming sword that came and stood in my vision. The sword stood with the hilt to the floor and the tip pointing upward. The fire on it glowed, and had continual movement. At first when I saw it, I thought that this must be something that I had seen before. I remembered seeing in a book that was given me, an angel holding a flaming sword. I thought at first that maybe this was just a memory of that moment.

But the sword stayed before my vision as I lay before the Lord and did not leave. It stayed for days. I was in a heart cry before the Lord. The prayer was "Lord, Come!" That was the extent to my prayer. It became a whisper of my heart before the Lord. Then the Lord caused me to remember a vision I had had, where I was before the throne of God and said, "Belieeeeeeeve!" I thought to say to the Lord, "This is your spoken word," at that moment something should have been created in me.

April 16, 2012

I had a dream that I was praying for people. A woman came up to me in the dream, and she had three spirits that looked just like her. The picture looked like a genie coming out of a bottle. They followed her wherever she went. She came up to me, and I asked her did she want to get saved. She said she was already saved. I asked her again and she was willing to pray the Sinner's prayer. As she did, the larger spirit wrapped her arms around the girl. I continued to pray for her and they all left her. I told her the Lord would use her, and He did.

April 20, 2012

Receiving the promises of your prophetic words:

I was asking the Lord why so many, including myself, have had all these words from the Lord, yet very few words come to pass. What we have not understood is that everything that the Lord is speaking is coming from what Heaven has in store for us. *Eyes have not seen...* The problem is that we hear a word from the Lord in our flesh, and we think that we are going to receive what Heaven's will is for us in our fallen nature. It will not happen. God showed me this in the vision that I had when I was before the throne of God, and God said, "BELIEEEEEEEVE!" and immediately I was taken out to a different throne room.

As I heard God say this, immediately my flesh came up in the face of what I heard Him say. For me, it was a spirit of failure and rejection. So I said within myself, *Great—I got kicked out because I did not believe!* I went before the Throne and I said, *Great—I have an audience, and they are making a judgment. I will cry mercy on my miserable life.* It was not until the scepter was handed to me that I finally lined up with what Heaven was saying. I was often puzzled by this vision, because my head said one thing yet my spirit-man cried out what I knew was accurate from the Lord. What I said was in line with what Heaven was wanting. Therein is the key. We must align our will with Heaven's will in order to receive our prophetic destiny.

The Father began to show me in creation He said, "Light *be!*" and light was, and it was GOOD IN HIS SIGHT. God had given us a free will and with that free will daily we could choose who we would serve. God does not override our free will of choice. When God said, "Belieeeeeeeve!" in my mind, creation should have taken place in me just as He said to the earth, "let there be water" and it was so. Why did faith just appear like that in me? The Father showed me He does not override our will, our choice. Choose ye this day who you will serve.

Nature is to teach us obedience to Heaven's will. The trees grow in perfect alignment with the sun. Plants have, as it were, little solar plants in them so that each leaf turns to the sun to get what it needs. In turn, those plants serve their purpose as the Father had designed it, to serve nature. This is Heaven's design. I saw that once man fell, everything in him fights Heaven's design. When the Spirit of God comes on the scene, our fallen nature and carnal ways fight God just as satan fights against God's ways (i.e. me hearing the Lord speak - that was my carnal nature hearing the word of the Lord)

What we must understand is that we have ways in us that have been discipled by satan: fear, failure, pride, arrogance, etc.. The Lord wants our spirit man to grow so that it can receive the kingdom. Our spirit man only grows when we pray, when we come into alignment with God. Scripture says that Jesus would often slip away to pray. He said, *My house shall be called a house of prayer.* The carnal man cannot receive the things of the spirit; they are foolishness to the carnal or natural man. If we choose our fleshly nature, then every prophetic word will be stolen from us. We will not see what the Lord has prepared for us. Our carnal nature will not receive what the Lord has for us when we receive a true prophetic word from someone.

The Father is saying, *My precious one, this is what I have prepared for you. This is your original design, your purpose on planet Earth. This is the abundant life I am calling you to. From my vantage point (Heaven's view) this is what I have laid up for you as an inheritance from Me, My beloved child. Now choose Me this day; I came that you might have life in abundance.*

If we choose Him, we grow closer in prayer and seeking. We begin to line up with His vision for us. He begins to disciple every way of satan out of us. He says, *My ways are not your ways.* Jesus said He learned obedience by the things that He suffered. As we pray out our prophecies and hold them up before the Lord, at times it seems like we are headed in a different direction than what the

Lord has spoken over us. He takes us the desert route, where things can look unfamiliar and even hostile.

Remember, Jesus went through the desert on the way to His destiny. We only stay on track with God through prayer. The church is filled with prayerlessness. The church wants to receive its next "word" to feel good about itself and say, "See? I am ok."

The Father is saying, *My precious child, this is My plan; this is My destiny. Now, begin to walk with Me, and you will receive it. Just trust Me.* Even as Jesus came to give us the abundant life, satan comes to steal, kill, and destroy what Heaven has for us. The only way to receive Heaven's destiny is to pray until we receive the promises. Don't just hear a word from God through the prophetic gifts. See it come to pass by walking with Him in a life filled with prayer. All things in the Word would come to pass as we pray.

Chapter 19

Signs of the Times

May 6, 2012

The Church is like Jonah, stuck in the belly of the whale and groping in darkness because they would not do it God's way. Jesus said, "The only sign that will be given is the sign of Jonah." This picture is the church standing in old, stagnant, smelly, fishy water. Standing in death rather than life, because it refuses to walk in God's vision for it and chooses instead its own imagination of God.

What sighted person would let a blind man describe a tree to him when he is looking at it in all of its size, color, and texture? So is a people without God's vision. God's heart cannot describe what is of His Spirit, unless we come out of darkness and walk in the light of the Lord. The sign of Jonah is throughout the land, as the people are in great darkness and do not know the ways of God. They do not believe the ones that the Lord has sent, because their understanding has become darkened out of disobedience to the truth. "The only sign that will be given is the sign of Jonah." Rebellion and hard-heartedness.

May 11, 2012

Seymour and I were in prayer. As we prayed, I saw the hands of God again. They were huge over us and glowed with His presence. Water came out of His hands, and poured over Seymour and me like a river. My eyes were opened and I saw flashes that came before me slowly. The first was a war in the Heavens.

I could not see the war, but knew there was one. I heard, *"Will you ride with me?"* Of course I said, "Yes, Lord!" I remembered how I would sing that song many times in church and my heart cried out, "Yes Lord, I will ride with you."

Then I heard that the angels I've met have personalities. I remembered meeting the Revival Angel of Charleston, who had a humble yet firm spirit. I thought of the Revival Angel of Washington DC's personality was serious and immovable. I was being told to go on an assignment that I was questioning. Very firmly, he pointed telling me to go. I knew I must obey. Of course, I always want to obey the Father's will anyway, so I do what I am told.

Then I saw Raphael, and he loved to dance and go to war dancing and rejoicing. He seemed majestic, somber, and light-hearted all at the same time. He carried a gold spear and a glowing shield. He would dance and beat His spear against his shield in a rhythmic sort of away. It was awesome to behold. He seemed both imposing and yet approachable and joyful.

Suddenly, I was no longer afraid of my visions. I felt great peace. My soul no longer fought me. I was not worried about what people would say about my visions. Knowing that I could see eternal things when others only saw temporal gave me a sense of release to embrace what God had chosen for me. So I forgot about people and their opinions.

Then I saw Seymour and myself take our place on the circumference of the earth. There were other men and women there as we joined them in the circle. Suddenly, I saw a lion that looked right at me, but I was not afraid. He was covered in eyes. I reached out and touched and patted him on his head. Next, I saw an eagle; he was covered in eyes as well. Then I saw an ox, then a man. They were all covered in eyes. Then I saw an angel with four wings. With two wings he covered the front of himself, and two wings went up in the air. This was a very restful vision. I saw all this in great peace as we prayed. Each scene flashed before my eyes. I started to sing, *Holy, holy, holy, is the Lord God almighty.* There was a peaceful feeling in the room.

May 17, 2012

I awoke this morning seeing that Jesus was wearing a linen garment which covered His head. He had on sandals. I was looking at the back of Him. He seemed tall in height. As He turned to me, His eyes were filled with pure light and that light shined into my heart.

June 12, 2012

As we were driving down the road, I suddenly saw a golden waterfall in the distance. I was looking in another place or realm of the spirit into a lush garden. The waterfall was made of pure, golden water. I never saw anything like this before; it was quite beautiful. I saw this waterfall many days. I got closer to the waterfall, and the water covered us all over. Several days later, I saw a silver waterfall. This one I saw from a side view, while I saw the golden waterfall from a frontal position.

June 19, 2012

We were at a pastors dinner and saw some old friends of ours who felt it was time to leave our church years earlier. Many members went with them. The Lord had given me a dream months before this had happened. I saw us in a new place. It was clean and bright. Everything was white—bright white. I saw a dome colonnade missing one column, and I knew that when this column was in place we were ready for whatever the Lord had planned for us. The column that needed to go in was forgiveness and loving people no matter what and to leave the judgment of others to the Lord.

When we saw this couple, I felt nothing but love for them. They had bad news to tell us about the church they started, and my heart wanted to weep with them, because we had been through the same thing with them and I knew how they felt. I reminded the brother that the sheep belong to God and we need to forgive offenses—it was the only way to get past them. I felt freedom doing it God's way. I thank God for this lesson. I began to praise God for all that we had been though—all the trials, the hurt, and pain. All the persecution and loss of relationships. I told the Lord, "You are all-wise. Thank you, Father."

June 19, 2012 (later)

Every night I would play Scripture on my phone so that the Word of God washed over us as Seymour and I went to sleep. This night I forgot to plug my phone in and turn the Word of God on. So I got up to get my phone, and as I did I saw a vision of Jesus. He was wearing a pure white robe that glowed white, and His feet were the color of bronze. I knew as I went to lie down and listen to the Word that the Lord was saying, *I have walked where you are walking; I have overcome, you will overcome as well.* I had been talking to the Lord earlier in the day about weaknesses, the things I would like to have victory over—annoying habits like watching too much TV, being too idle with my time, needing more focus on the Lord and His will, etc.. He was showing He had overcome this world and its traps, and that I will overcome because of Him. Praise God, He is faithful.

June 24, 2012

As I lay in prayer, I saw a map of the earth come into my vision. The map was a line graph of the earth. First it was straight up, then it lay flat. It moved back and forth, then it came closer. Suddenly, I found myself looking at South America. As I got closer, it got clearer and became 3D. I continued to move in, then actually moved into the map, where I saw a jungle and people who were sick. They were lying on the ground everywhere, sick and dying. I looked on a map later and saw it was Uruguay, South America. *(Note: Although not confirmed of the Lord at this time, this may be the Zika virus which started in South America in 2016.)*

There is a young man who came to Messiah's Church (our church) who knew nothing about what had happened before with our prayerwalk. I had made banners, each with a specific significance. Some were for intimacy, some for the nations, etc.. We often wave these banners before the Lord in prayer, calling out to God to come in this form or another. This young man took each banner that I had made. There were a lot of other banners in the basket, but he picked each one I had personally made (without realizing it) and started to go throughout the church and wave them before the Lord. I saw him and knew He had each one.

The Lord spoke, and said every prayer was heard. Not one thing would fall to the ground. I began to weep because I knew God had remembered us and we were not forgotten by Him. He had heard our hearts' cry, He heard the many years of prayer and intercession that went up before Him.

What an amazing time of worship it was; God came down in such a beautiful way, and His presence filled the place. I saw golden bags in the air over everyone. They needed to do nothing except simply receive what the Lord had for them.

July 15-17, 2012

We went to our fourth gate. The location was "Ground Zero" in New York. Before we went, our son, Joseph, felt like he needed to be baptized. I believe this was prophetic, as I know that the Lord is about to baptize His people. Some for deeper service, and some for true change of heart.

Our New York Trip

We have finished our first level of assignment to New York.

Wow, what God moments we had! We were sent to speak to the rulers and princes over New York, to declare the coming move of God. We prayed at Ground Zero, then we went to a church on that site. Their services were being held in the 7th World Trade Center on the 40th floor at Ground Zero, where part of the events of 9/11 took place. The church was afraid of tomorrow, the speaker was giving a motivational message about getting a job. As I watched him, after a while his eye sockets began to glow red. It was very strange to me. I asked Seymour if he seeing what I saw. This went on the whole time he spoke.

The people did not enter into praise and worship. They stood because they were told to. Few were singing or responding to the songs. They had prayer before the service, and said they never do this, but someone suggested instead of asking God what *we* want, let's ask God what *He* wants. Once that was spoken, our assignment began to unfold from Lord Holy Spirit (they were trying to stir the prophetic gifts). They named various things, like someone was bitten by a tick, someone had back pain, etc., and the worship leader said that if these things fit you, to go over to the corner where the prayer team could pray for you. After a time of worship, he said, "We have never done this before, but if anyone wants to pray out loud, please feel free to pray. Only pray really loud so that all can hear you pray."

One man prayed, speaking very softly, then there was silence. At this point, I heard the quickening of God the Father in my spirit. He told me to pray, to obey the worship leader and pray really loud (God was about to speak prophetically to New York city at Ground Zero what must be held to in faith). I raised my hands to the Lord, and with a loud voice proclaimed His words over this church, which was named The River Church. I began to pray that this church would become a river that could not be stopped, and that the young people that were there (the place was filled with young people from all nationalities) would know Jesus intimately; that they would have a face to face encounter with Him. I prayed that the glory of the Lord would rest in that place; that they would be ablaze for Jesus, and be light in that dark place. The presence of God would rest at Ground Zero and people would be drawn to that place because of the light of His presence. I prayed for a move of God to take New York.

When I finished, they quickly ended the service and no one looked at Seymour or me. Everyone scattered from the room, and even the pastor turned his back to us. The words were not what they wanted, yet they had asked God what did *He* want. God sent us to answer the prayer they prayed before the

service began. Afterward, the Lord spoke to us clearly to get out of the city. We would normally visit family that live in the area as we headed back, but we were told to go home without stopping anywhere on the way. We later saw why, as a great storm came over New York.

Excerpts from *The Blaze* July 19, 2012: *"Some have compared the storm that occurred yesterday over New York City and in other areas of the northeast as to that of Biblical proportions. The Weather Channel reports that the extremely hot and humid day within the city came to a violent and abrupt end as the storm erupted in the late afternoon..."...*Characterized by hail, heavy winds and torrential rain, the storm in New York has produced stunning photographs, which led Gizmodo to jokingly wonder if the Lost Ark of the covenant was opened in NYC or if the Ghostbusters were back in town.

"Powerful summer storm brings torrential rain, quarter-size hailstones and ground-shaking thunder to New York City. Twitter users posted photographs of an apocalyptic storm cloud that appeared to be swallowing up the metropolis, including a dramatic one that showed the city seemingly engulfed by a funnel."

Photos by Dhani Jones, NY Daily

I guess when we ask God a question we need to listen for the answer, and receive what He sends. For us, it was awesome because we were found in His will. The sure word of the Lord spoken at Ground Zero in absolute faith of what God intends had been delivered. The story of New York City unfolds from here. The fourth city is prepared for God's Spear. The fifth city comes!

July 18, 2012

As I was waking up, I saw a tremendous wall of water coming toward me. It was a tsunami, a furious wave that consumed everything in its way. It came close and towered over me, and I realized it was a prophetic picture of what God is getting ready to do in the land. It was a picture of the coming move of God. Praise the Lord, we are getting closer to the times of His moving over the land. PREPARE YOUR HEARTS! This move will be like nothing we have experienced before. It may not be a "make me feel good" or "heal me" move; it will not be a soft spring rain but instead it will be a powerful, cleansing force that will be for *His* glory. This move will be a "line up with His will and His heart" move.

> *"He is coming," says the Lord of hosts. "But who can endure the day of His coming? And who can stand when He appears? For He is like a refiner's fire and*

like fullers' soap. 3 He will sit as a smelter and purifier of silver, and He will purify the sons of Levi and refine them like gold and silver, so that they may present to the Lord offerings in righteousness (Mal 3:2-3).

July 28, 2012

It was the first time in a while that the Lord had sent us out to minister. We were in a new place with Him, and He was sending us in a different manner than He had before. I knew we were being offered the same things others were offered that went before us. First, the temptation to yield to the needs of the people rather than listen acutely to God and what He wanted to say to them. Second was the offering—we were not to be concerned about what came in as financial reward. Instead, we were to cast our crowns before the feet of Jesus; give all the glory to Him. We must cast down our crowns before the King of Glory.

July 31, 2012

As Seymour and I lay before the Lord to pray, I saw the Revival Angel of Charleston. I thanked the Lord for the blessing of letting me meet Him. I saw the bowl of prayer and worship He gave me. He then handed me a beautiful golden key with *Philadelphia* written on it. How the Lord wants to give us all things.

August 16, 2012

I saw a huge tsunami about three feet away from me. I knew this tsunami had already hit us all. I saw a waterfall of fire begin to flow, and then a wind blowing. I knew these were three calamities that were going to hit the earth.

At our ladies meeting, we began to pray. I had been praying for prayers that cause travail. This is something that can't be worked up, but is instead the work of Lord Holy Spirit praying through you. We prayed about two hours, and the spirit of travail fell on all that were there during that time. At the end of prayer, I heard the Lord say that what I was praying for was done. He said, *Now, listen to the tears of Heaven.* Suddenly, there was a downpour of rain. The weight of water that fell was surreal, soaking everything in a moment of time. I listened for ten minutes to the rain fall, when I heard the Lord say, *"It would take these many tears to stop what I am going to do upon the land."* I knew that if I cried my whole life, I could not cry enough tears to match the rain that fell in that one hour. It would take the whole world to cry out to stop the hand of God.

The great thing about anything the Lord does is it always brings the beautiful fruit of righteousness and peace afterwards. Someone must stand in the gap and suffer for the weight of sin so that others go free—Jesus was our example of that. One generation must be purged that another can go free. Our children will inherit the ways of God; we repent so that they walk closer with God. So don't fear, instead trust God above all things. This is a time of great miracles! Daniel was used of God to save his nation. They still went into exile, yet Daniel and his friends had great miraculous deliverance from the Lord of Glory.

Get ready, we are going to see it again! Our God is great, and though He slay me, yet will I trust Him and forever praise His name! *Say to the righteous that it shall be well with them, for they shall eat the fruit of their deeds (Isaiah 3:10).*

Chapter 20

Joy in the Midst of the Storm

August 18, 2012

As we were worshiping at the "Prophets Gathering," the Lord said, *"In order to get through this time, you must rejoice."* I saw a large, fierce whirlwind in the room, and as we were worshiping, the whirlwind dissipated. The Lord was saying as we worship and praise Him—though the storms of life are all around us, seeking to destroy everything we know as life—that the storm will dissolve right in front of us. The Lord confirmed the word, saying, *"The heavens will be shaken, and when you see these things, look up and rejoice, for your redemption draws near."*

Seymour was awakened by the Lord. He was given a teaching about rejoicing in Him in troubling times. On Sunday, a friend of ours was ministering with us and He spoke on Romans 1:12: *Because they did not honor and thank me...*These were three witnesses the Lord gave about rejoicing in Him. It is time to rejoice in the Lord.

August 21, 2012

I had been seeing two travelers for days, but I did not understand what I was seeing. This time I paid attention, and I noticed the travelers were walking in a straight line. One in the front and one was behind him. The one in the front was full of light, I could not see Him. But I could clearly see the one that was following. He had a linen garment on that was brownish tan.

August 24, 2012

I had a dream vision, where I was not fully awake, yet not asleep. I saw the circumference of the earth. I was looking at the horizon, and the sky was blue with beautiful clouds. In the air was a huge puddle of black oily water that began to drip downward. As one drop dripped down, it filled the whole beautiful blue sky with darkness. It was half black and half blue as darkness seeped down over the earth. There was not a star in the sky, only blackness.

August 26, 2012

I saw the earth and it looked like someone was shaking it, like you would shake a snow globe to get all the snow to cover the model inside.

August 27, 2012

I saw a place where there was rubble everywhere; buildings were knocked down in a heap. It looked bad—a natural disaster had taken place, similar to what it looks like when a tornado hits leaving the area in shambles"

August 30, 2012

As we prayed this night I was resting in the Lord. I heard singing. I heard singing. The sound was soft and beautiful, yet constant. At first I thought it was the wind, but the sound continued for a few minutes and I thought *this is a sound of Heaven*. It was beautiful and unrelenting. Then it stopped for a moment. The Lord had opened my ears, and I was listening to Heaven singing.

August 31, 2012

I awoke early this morning. As soon as my eyes were slightly opened, I heard singing. This time the singing was louder than the night before. I could hear it with clarity and the sound was beautiful. I heard, as it were a great choir. Millions were singing a song to the Lord. Every now and then there were horns joining the song that resounded in my ears. Again, my natural mind engaged and I thought perhaps it was the Word that was playing in my ears. I was able to separate the sounds. Surely it was the sounds of Heaven.

Then I saw an army with banners. Jesus led the charge; they were all on white horses. The horses were beings within themselves. They were as Scripture describes them—mighty and powerful, full of the life and power of God. The banners were beautiful, all of them were white and they waved softly as the wind blew upon them. The army carried the banners of righteousness. Everyone on the horses was dressed in white and gold. This was the Lord and His host.

I fell asleep again, and went into a dream. In the dream, I was on a bus that was carrying people from different walks of life. I knew some of the people, and we were casually talking about various things concerning the Lord. I had some pills used for fallout from a nuclear blast. I only had enough for Seymour and me. Yet it was a big bag of pills. I thought maybe I should share them so that others could survive with us. We would not survive long if we did this, because what we had could only take care of us. We needed to take the full dosage.

> *The foolish said to the prudent, 'Give us some of your oil, for our lamps are going out.' But the prudent answered, 'No, there will not be enough for us and you too; go instead to the dealers and buy some for yourselves (Matt 25:8,9).*

There was a woman outside the bus. I suddenly reached out and grabbed her and pulled her onto the bus. The moment I pulled her in, a stone fell from the sky. I picked up the stone and saw that it looked like a meteor. It was gray, very hard and had holes in it. Somehow, I took this stone and the pills and hid them in a hole in a building the bus had passed. We were on the bus for a while, then stopped at the same building where I had hid the stone and the pills. I pulled them out and brought them on the bus with me again. The person in charge of the bus motioned to all that got off too quickly to get on and not hesitate. I jumped on and took my first round of pills. Again I thought about giving some to the others on the bus so that they, too, could survive.

I walked to the front of the bus to see a sight that was so frightening that I could not believe my eyes. I saw buildings toppling over, including water towers that were on high platforms (like the water towers that are at the entrance of cities), all being destroyed. All the towers that were high in the air were being thrown down to the ground by a huge wall of water. The bus driver was trying to avoid the oncoming wave, swerving the bus from right to the left. I watched in horror as a red train wrapped itself around one of the water towers. All at once, it was falling to the ground, both train and water tower. I was yelling "JESUS,

JESUS!" I wanted to go to the back of the bus and hide my face, to close my eyes so that I would not see what was going to happen next. But something inside me knew I needed to stand there and see the destruction that was taking place. I stood there screaming in terror, "JESUS, JESUS!" I woke up.

Both the vision and the dream are a part of each other. The vision of Heaven is what is taking place from Heaven's point of view. Heaven is rejoicing because the kingdoms of this world are becoming the kingdoms of our Lord. Jesus is coming with His army to make all things right. He is coming to put things in order from Heaven's point of view.

In the dream I was preparing for a disaster, and like the story of the five wise virgins, I knew I needed to hold onto my supply of pills. Like the virgins who would not have had enough oil for both themselves and others who had not prepared, I wanted to help others, but each person needed their own supply. In the dream, I saved a lady that a rock was going to fall on. Scripture says to fall on the rock before the rock falls on you. The bus was a vehicle of protection. We were protected but it was still a fearful thing to see. The train represented denominations and fivefold ministries.

Steps of Understanding
(Interpretation):

I believe this dream was about the stored things of God that we think we have and know concerning God's ways. (Water represents the spirit, the things of God we think we have fully learned). These ideas will be toppled by the presence of God. Buildings and denominations that have built high towers will be brought down. This will be a terrible thing, because belief systems will be shaken. What we thought we knew about God will be dethroned by the reality of who He is in His character nature.

I believe the singing and rejoicing in the heavens, and the scene of the Lord and His host was a prelude to the dream. He is coming to show His people who He really is. He is coming as a righteous King. This is why we must love Him more than life itself. Who can stand in the day of His coming? Those that love Him with their whole heart. The fear of the Lord will be established once again and His ways made known. Each person must save himself in that day. It will be the day of the Lord.

Chapter 21

Edicts from the Courts of Heaven

September 20, 2012

The Lord awoke me early this morning and my heart was full of prayer. I heard Him say the night before, *"Will you stand in the gap for the people and make up the hedge?"* I remembered the word the Lord spoke to me about how we were made out of defective material, and how we were quick to fall into sin. I acknowledged my Adamic nature, and I said, "Yes, Lord, You have had mercy on me so many times. Can I not have mercy and grace for others?" I got up and began to cry out to God with all my heart, asking for the Lord for a baptism that would change all things.

He began to show me those in the Word who found the ancient foundation once it was lost. He showed me Enoch. Enoch walked with God as Adam did, and God took him. I knew that we needed to have a walk like Enoch had.

October 11, 2012

We were on our assignment to the fifth city, Philadelphia. The week before, we had met with a sister who told us to get in touch with a certain group of people in Philadelphia. She has been behind the scenes on many moments, preceding much of what Seymour and I have been involved with.

We went to the meeting they were having in Media, PA, where the leader of the group played his keyboard under the inspiration of the Holy Spirit. He could hear sounds in the spirit as people prayed in tongues. As Seymour and I sang in the Spirit, he said he went to a new place in the Spirit he had never been to before. The sound was incredible. We were amazed at his playing. There was also a man there who had a humble spirit. The Lord had told him to move to Philadelphia from Oklahoma City. He uprooted his family and obeyed the Lord. The Lord told him there would be revival in Philadelphia.

We spent the next day with him, as he took us on a tour of Valley Forge. He shared with us that George Washington had a word from an angel who told him there would always be a union. Before he told us this, I was seeing an angel. She was dressed in white and the wind was blowing her dress. I heard there would be war and revival—in that order. I asked God to confirm this. As the man was speaking to us, the wind began to blow. The air had been still before this moment. I knew I was seeing and hearing what the Lord was saying to me. We later observed that nations are often referred to as "she," or "her." I believe that is why I saw a female angel.

(I want to take a moment here to declare that our nation is claimed as the property of GOD the Father.)

Later that evening, we were given a book from a descendant of George Washington who had written about his forefather's encounter with a feminine gender angel. The brother leading the tour did not know I was seeing the angel, nor had he told me the angel was supposedly feminine that George Washington had seen. We trust the Lord in His leading, so encounters have His parameters and understandings for what lies ahead, not ours. We left our new friend, and went on our assignment which was to "STRIKE THE GROUND," and speak the word "RETURN." I heard the words, "AWAKEN, ARISE AND RETURN!"

We arrived there at 8 PM. The Lord had taken us to Valley Forge for His purposes, then sent us into the city at night, incognito, Joshua/Caleb style, traveling through bumper-to-bumper traffic to our destination, to arrive exactly at EIGHT o'clock. We noticed this because as soon as our tires hit the city ground, the bells rang out over Independence Hall eight times. Seymour and I looked at each other. We knew it was a sign from the Lord of something new, beginning, again—GOD in sovereign control of even the most minor moment.

Who could have thought leaving early that morning, being ordered of the Lord to spend the day with one of the gatekeepers of Philadelphia, hearing stories about George Washington and the hand of the Lord upon our nation, we would arrive at our assigned plot of ground at exactly 8:00 where bells would ring over Independence Hall, the old city hall, and the President's house where Washington and Adams lived from 1790 to 1800. Surely, the Lord our God intends to speak to the covenant He made with our nation, created for His purposes.

We went behind the large granite monument that stated the first amendment to the Constitution about religious freedom. We struck the ground many times and we cried, "RETURN, CHURCH, RETURN, LAND! AWAKEN, ARISE AND RETURN, CHURCH, TO THE ORIGINAL FOUNDATIONS OF THE LORD!"

Earlier, we had the man whom the Lord had sent to the city pray for us. As he prayed, I saw that as we struck the ground of the fifth city, the ground opened up all the way from Philadelphia to Charleston, SC. It looked like a huge fissure in the earth. The hole was big and had cracks all around it that went in many directions. From the edge of the hole in Philadelphia, Seymour and I turned into a mighty Lion and we roared with a mighty roar down the east coast. I could hear the sound of that roar, and it was fierce. The man that was praying over us began to prophesy what I was seeing. The fifth city is done in its beginnings. All five cities have had the word of the Lord spoken on a "spot of ground."

Get ready, America. Come forth, Church of the Living GOD. GOD the Father has prepared a way. It's HIS TIME Now—Are you ready to run? *(Note: the brother we met said, "God was going to grant to us the gift of faith. He did not give that gift to many people because they could not be trusted with it. But that God would give it to us and we would move in it freely.")*

October 23, 2012

I awoke from a dream that was scary and wonderful. Seymour and I and various other people were waist deep in the ocean, and we were all playing. I had a white tube that gave off a sweet fragrance. I had placed the tube in one of the rooms we had, a women who goes to our church said that she took it out of the room because the smell was too overpowering and she did not like it. She had it in her hands and she was showing it to us.

When she said this, the ocean drew back, and I saw a pile of dead fish. At this point I yelled, "RUN!" just as the water came forward with great force. I was running as fast as I could, and did not see who else was running or who survived. As I ran, I thought "Lord, if I keep running and take a deep breath before the water hits, I will survive and swim to the top of the wave!" As I was thinking this, I glanced quickly over my shoulder to see the water at my heels. I felt the spray of the water at my back, and then the wind picked me up, right to the top of the wave. I could see Seymour, he was still running. He kept looking back, and I knew he was looking to see where I was. He was way out in front of the wave, still running and looking back for me. I saw that the wind had blown all of his clothes off, and he had on red and white underwear. I kept waving at him so that he could see I was safe. I was at the top of the wave and moving forward with it. The wind gently put me down and I ran up to Seymour and hugged him. We were safe. Then he turned and spoke out, "Put your anchor in!"

The meaning of the dream is this: We are walking with the Lord in some things, because we were walking waist deep in the ocean. We have a fragrance that is the Lord, but for some it is too strong, so it is being rejected. The words are too strong for them, so they are removing the fragrance from their heart, or the Word from their hearts, and giving it back to us, saying, "I don't want that." This causes the spirit of God or the water of God to gain fury, because they were not rejecting us—they were rejecting the Lord. God began to uncover all things so that they could be seen for what and who they are. The fish were dead, meaning the water was all around the fish but the fish were not taking in the water of God. In other words, the spirit of God is all around people and leaders but they are not walking it out, they are not walking *in* it, and are in the spirit dead.

The water is coming out of its place and going forth where it would not normally be, on lands and peoples. To some it will be a crushing, to others it will lift them up high to ride the Spirit and move with Him. He will be gentle to those that trust Him and they will be safe. He will uncover all things so that we will know who is Holy and who is not. He will have His prophets speak His word of the hour, in this case, "Put your anchor in." We are living in times that are about to become more tumultuous than ever before in history. You MUST be anchored in Christ now, for a wave is coming—*and who can endure this day?*

October 28, 2012

I was leading worship at a gathering called "Panim El Panim" which means face-to-face in Hebrew. This is a yearly gathering that takes place. People come from all over the states and the world to this conference. As I was leading worship and focusing on the Lord, I Suddenly saw a white horse over my head. Jesus was seated on the horse; He was the King that led a host. The horse was fierce in his appearance. He was ready to go in any direction the Lord would point him to go. The Lord had a sword in His hand; He was pointing the sword in specific directions. I saw Him point the sword towards two areas in front of Him. He also pointed in a third direction, but I did not see this direction. I only sensed it. In front of Jesus and the horse was darkness, great darkness. It looked like the hordes of hell. I saw the Lord charge forward and a host followed them. All this went right over my head as I looked up. I was underneath this great army moving forward. I felt a shaking. It was a tremendous shaking, I began to shake my hand. My hand shook without control. Then I heard a gavel. I had my staff and I began to strike my staff to the ground, mimicking the sound I heard. Suddenly I became God's gavel, I became the Gavel of God. I began to jump. I became one with my staff as I jumped. I then began to say, "Court is in session. Come to order, the King has sat down to judge!"

After all this, I lay before the Lord. I was at the throne of God, standing on the right. Then I said, "Look!" and I saw the earth. It looked like a marble. Then I saw lights with clouds trailing behind them, moving and covering the whole earth until I could no longer see the earth. All that could be seen was the cloud with lights moving inside of it. I knew these lights, covered by His glory, were doing various things in the earth. *The glory of the Lord will cover the earth as the water covers the sea.* I knew this glory was not to be used for our own purposes, although all glory is a joy to those who walk with Him. Those that were not with Him became afraid. The earth became different. It was covered in a cocoon and was being made new.

November 22, 2012

As Seymour and I were praying, I began to strike my staff on the ground and command the way to open up before us. I said, "Open up Red Sea, open every door before us!" I then saw myself giving birth. I was looking down, I had on a white dress that was covering my knees. I was laying on my back looking down at my knees. I thought I would see a baby, but instead I saw a large bubble float up. I heard, "Restore the way of the Lord. Teach the ancient ways of the Lord."

November 25, 2012

It was a Sunday and Seymour was ministering the word in Psalms 91. About 45 minutes into the message, I saw the room get bright. It was getting brighter as he spoke; the Lord had opened my eyes to see what was happening in the spirit. He had just finished reading about the angels bearing you up in their hands. He spoke of the angels the Lord had given to us; he was calling them by name and testifying of what the Lord was saying.

November 29, 2012

While in prayer I had some questions for the Lord. I asked Him why we had to go through all that we had gone through. What was the purpose, what was the plan? As I was lying down, I thought of Job and then Jacob. I remembered how they contended with the Lord. In Job's case, he wondered why he went through what came upon him. His friend said it was because he had sinned and was not faithful. They came up with many reasons why he was suffering. Yet, when the Lord showed up, He said they lacked understanding; and He reprimanded Job for asking God his question. I am sure Job did not care about being reprimanded. He was glad He showed up with relief and an answer. He was glad to repent.

Jacob grabbed hold of the angel and would not let go until he blessed him. I knew we needed to grab hold until we saw the blessing. As I began to fall asleep, the Lord said to me softly, "I made them vulnerable." I realized that Job had nothing—his house and all that he had was taken from him. He had no protection but the Lord. He sat in ashes, praying for death. When Jacob wrestled with the angel, he touched his hip socket and made him lame. He was vulnerable, going into a new land with women and children. The Lord made sure they knew He was their protector even though they faced many things.

December 9, 2012

Father God told me to go tell a person close to us that the Lord was going to judge all disobedience and He needed to repent to the Lord and turn from all disobedience and get himself ready. He needed to repent and run to the Lord. I heard the Lord say there would be a famine of the Word yet the Spirit of Prophecy was going to fall on His prophets. I felt like the word out of the true prophets was going to run like water, a word that is new. A word that moved with God, but it was the WORD of the LORD. Not fluffy words that tickled us but a word of direction that needed to be stepped into. I know that Israel will step in and lead the charge of the prophetic. These prophets would be different than what we are used to; they will be no-nonsense. Things spoken will come to pass. They would be like men of old speaking THE WORD OF THE LORD. I knew I needed to prepare. I had had a dream on 10/23/12 (concerning the tsunami and the dead fish), and this day—48 days later—this dream began to come to pass. Help Lord! I saw that God was uncovering all the dead things in His house. This has already begun and is continuing. I do not want to judge the Lord's body. Because it is evident by the way things are and the inability for people to truly hear the Lord.

December 12, 2012

It was midnight and I was getting ready for bed. I was talking to the Lord about giftings and asking if He would give Seymour and me gifts from Him. I immediately saw a beautiful blue and magenta gift box, wrapped in a white bow and being handed down to me from above. I saw myself reach up and take the box. I was listening to the Word as I was going to sleep. A passage in Deuteronomy was describing the special abilities God had given His workers to create the different parts of the tabernacle and to teach others how to do it as well. I asked the Lord for special abilities to do His will and to be able to teach them to others.

January 13, 2013

Seymour and I were in prayer. We were praying about various things, holding them up before the Lord. I suddenly saw Jesus. We were in a garden, and He had on a white robe and burgundy draping shawl around His shoulders. I seemed to focus on His feet and the sandals He wore, which were brown. Jesus sat down on a white bench that was in the form of a semi-circle. Not a half circle, but a quarter circle. As He sat down I saw He had a brown book with the name "Secrets" written on it. He told me to use one of the keys I was given earlier (from the keys I received when I was on the conveyer belt.) I took the key and opened the book. When I did, light flooded out of the book and poured all over me. I saw the word "Faith" on the first page of the book.

January 1, 2013
I sat down with Seymour to study, and I heard this word from Isaiah 10:5: *Woe to Assyria, the rod of My anger, and the staff in whose hands is My indignation.* I knew that the Lord was talking about Syria and related countries and that at some point we would see Damascus reduced to rubble (Amos 1:3).

January 2, 2013
I believe how we will grow is through salvations. Many in the church will not step into the new that God is doing, therefore, He has saved a generation that will. The newly saved will come and learn how to walk with God without the taint of religion. He is raising a people out of darkness to fully walk in His glorious light. As Seymour talked about the glory of the Lord, I saw an army on horseback. They started to move forward slowly, many with banners blowing in the wind. They were standards that were coming from Heaven. God was coming in a new way to Earth.

January 12, 2013
I want to give you an awesome testimony of praise. My husband and I were in prayer a few nights ago. We were praying about different things and lifting various people up before the Lord. The Lord had been speaking to me about faith and believing Him no matter what was going on around me. I had faith on some levels, but on other levels I saw that I actually only had *hope* in God. Like all of us, we find we have a need so we pray and hope God will move and things will turn out as we hope they will. As Seymour and I prayed this time, the sound of the prayer was different. The Lord spoke to me and said, *"Faith has a sound, and when I hear the sound of faith in you, things will begin to change."* The sound was

steadfast and unmoving. This "sound of faith" recognized and honored who the Father is and who we are in relationship to Him. This was a glorious moment. The sound had rest in it and a quiet strength; it was more than words can convey. But I heard it. I now can recognize and identify it. This faith has the ability to move mountains and walk with The Father. To me, this is the pearl of great price. My faith has been tested many times. I have stood in ignorance not knowing what was going on. I now know every word we pray to the Lord has incense. That incense has a sound; it's our faith full of worship to the HOLY ONE. I know we are on the verge of the greatest move of God the world has ever known and we will need such faith to step into it.

> *And these attesting signs will accompany those who believe: in My name they will drive out demons; they will speak in new languages; They will pick up serpents; and [even] if they drink anything deadly, it will not hurt them; they will lay their hands on the sick, and they will get well (Mark 16:17-18 AMP).*

> *When He had taken the book, the four living creatures and the twenty- four elders fell down before the Lamb, each one holding a harp and golden bowls full of incense, which are the prayers of the saints. And they sang a new song, saying, "Worthy are You to take the book and to break its seals; for You were slain, and purchased for God with Your blood men from every tribe and tongue and people and nation. You have made them to be a kingdom and priests to our God; and they will reign upon the earth (Rev 5:8-10).*

January 20, 2013

We were worshipping at church. I was holding my staff which I had redone as the Holy Spirit showed me. Suddenly, I was before the throne of God with my staff in my right hand. The Lord touched my staff without touching it. I then turned into my staff. I was now looking at my staff standing to the left side observing what was going on. Suddenly, appearing next to my staff was a straight line of staffs in front of the throne going off into eternity. I got up and told what I saw; when I did, I saw an unending amount of gifts come into my mouth. These gifts kept coming; they were all white and different sizes.

January 25, 2013

We were in Spartanburg, and I was leading worship. As all were singing, I could see four tiers of horses bowing before the Lord. They were beautifully majestic, and they bowed as though the King of Glory was about to come into the room. Later, a man testified seeing an army of the Lord with swords that shined so brightly. All the soldiers were bowing, and all the horses were bowing-both horse and rider. Then Jesus came in riding on a horse. The man said it was a glorious sight. This confirmed what I had seen.

January 26, 2013

We were conducting a meeting in Spartanburg. We were praying over breakfast when I saw the face of Jesus. I saw from His head to His shoulders. He wore a golden crown and a white tunic with white embroidery around the neckline and a sash of purple around His shoulders. Jesus was smiling at me. He seemed to be resting, as His shoulders were relaxed and back.

January 27, 2013

We had gotten in late from the meetings that were being held in Spartanburg and Greenville. It was 2:30 AM, and I was lying on my bed talking to the Lord about being persecuted and how to go through it. *"Many leaders do not believe the things that I have seen, Lord. They think I am seeing some false visions or drumming up some fantasy. After all, they have not seen any fruit out of the stories I have been telling them."* Suddenly, I saw Raphael. He was glowing, especially his hair. I had learned I was to approach him like any other servant of God. His voice was deep and he said, "Keep writing down your visions; this is very important." I said, "What about the persecutions? He touched my heart and put strength in it. I knew he had more to say, but I did not have enough strength to hear it yet.

January 30, 2013

It was a Wednesday night home group and Seymour asked us to go and stand before the Lord. I immediately went before the Throne and heard the Lord say, *"Now hear the Word of the Lord. I will raise you up and I will bring you out!"*

January 31, 2013

We had two ladies come over to talk about taking the "holy city" (Charleston, SC). I was watching Seymour and he was talking to them. I was wondering why he was standing over them, when I thought it would be better to sit to talk with them. As he stood there, I suddenly saw him dressed in silver armor. This armor was glowing and full of light. I then saw applets on his shoulders and they were pure gold. I knew he was a soldier of the King.

February 19, 2013

This Sunday was awesome again as people gave their hearts to the Lord. The Spirit of deliverance broke out over the people as they began to throw cigarettes and various sins on the communion plate. At our youth group, those that had gotten saved weeks before were now receiving the Holy Spirit with the evidence of speaking in tongues.

February 22, 2013

Seymour was giving the message from Exodus 19:5-6. I looked at the scripture and then read Exodus 19:9. I saw where the Lord said He would cover Moses with a cloud, and the people would believe. Then I saw Seymour and me covered in fire from the Lord. We were ablaze for Jesus and everything around us was set on fire for the Lord. We had gathered to pray and seek the Lord. We knew it was the time of the Father's move and we needed to prepare for persecution and wolves. We needed to keep our eyes upon the Lord's heart. He will take care of His people. We must be always teaching them to hear Him and walk with Him.

As we prayed, the Lord said, *Get your staff and pray.* I prayed and the Lord said that the prayer was bigger than our local church. He had me pray for all the spears that He had shown me last year that fell to the ground. I saw them like seeds that went into the ground, and it was time for them to germinate and begin to come forth. He said to call them forth in each of the cities where we had gone.

The Lord told me to knight each person in the room. They were being knighted as prayer warriors. I then could hear that some felt concerns of unworthiness about their relationship with the Lord. I looked around the room and I saw one sister for whom the Lord was pouring oil and water into her hands. Several angels of the Lord were ministering to everyone, letting them know they were accepted in the Lord. I knew that we all needed to learn that it was Him, and Him alone. It was not based on who we are. We needed to rest in that. I could see Seymour as a mature warrior; he has learned to keep his eyes on the Lord, not look to the right or the left nor look to himself. I also felt to pray for the new believers that would come.

February 23, 2013

We were at a cabin in the mountains of North Carolina. We did not realize that we needed a rest until someone offered the cabin to us. The Lord spoke to me this was Him, and that we needed to go. On this night the winds were blowing so loud that it reminded me of when the Lord told David to go into battle, "when you hear the wind in the mulberry trees."

The wind was so loud it woke Seymour and me both. I thought, *this is the sound of the Lord.* It was both frightening and thrilling at the same time. I began to pray upon being awakened by the wind. It was in the early morning hours, and I sought God about our situation, pouring out my heart to the Lord.

It may have sounded like a complaint. As I complained the wind would stop. As I repented, I noticed that the wind would pick up again. The Lord was gracious to me in the midst of my despair. I began to thank Him over and over, and I kept thinking, *this is the sound of the Lord.* How mighty the wind resounded in the trees. Then, as I was just about to fall asleep, I saw myself with two lightning bolts coming down to rest on my shoulders. They left a rectangle shaped, white silvery block on each of my shoulders. I was being given a rank. Like a lieutenant receives his bars, I was receiving a sign of rank in the Kingdom. I heard the word *epaulets.*

March 12, 2013

I was thinking upon the Lord and found myself again in the garden with the Lord. He was sitting, looking in the Book called Secrets. The book was lit up and glowing. I walked around to His right side as He was looking at the book and realized He was on the third page. I looked at it with Him. I knew we were walking in the third page. This page was about walking in rank and file.

March 17, 2013

As I was lying on my bed, I was praying all night long, sleeping in between prayers. We had a visitor over and he was up all night, under attack by a spirit that came in the room and pressed his head into the bed. This demonic spirit was on him so heavy that he had to get up on all fours to break its hold. The night before, he had rebuked a witchcraft spirit on a woman, and he was suffering backlash. It created a spirit of prayer in the house; we all felt it and were praying through the night.

At around 5 AM, I awoke into a vision where I saw a long table with Jesus standing at the end of it. The table was set with beautiful place settings. I was at the other end with two figures sitting on either side of me. They were black in color. I heard a scripture: *He prepares a table before us in the presence of our enemies.*

Earlier that day, we were visited by a young lady who had a deep spirit of unforgiveness in her life. She had been abused by many men and had endured traumatic circumstances. We were facing a person with demons that had a legal right to oppress her, so the enemy was not going to sit idle and let us rebuke him. He had her bound by her choices, and we had stepped on to his turf. There were two demons in particular we were fighting against: bitterness and witchcraft. We were both being attacked by these spirits. The Lord was using this vision to let us know not to worry; He had prepared a place of victory for us. We were going to eat from the table of His presence that always brings the victory. Only those obedient to the will of God can eat from His table. The others can only observe the victory that the Lord brings.

March 20, 2013

I went before the Courts of Heaven and prayed for Seymour and myself. We were going through a rough time. It seemed as if hell came against us—we were under attack about our home and other things. We were being heavily oppressed and were not sure where the next hit would come from. I was praying against the spirit of witchcraft, asking how they could have such power and authority against us. I began to pray and call out to the Father.

Suddenly, I saw two men enter the room. The thing that distinguished one of the men was the golden sash he wore across his chest. The sash looked heavy, draping low on his body. I had never seen anything like it. He had a clipboard in his hand and he was writing things; there seemed to be scaffolding above him. I believe he was charged with building things; he was like a head foreman, and he had a helper.

March 24, 2013

I started to lead worship and I saw blue lightning flash all over the church. The Father moved greatly. Two people gave their hearts to the Lord, and many were strengthened in Him. I believe the blue lightning was the Lord coming and gathering His people from every tribe, those that would be saved. It's the time of the ingathering. The Father is gathering those that are His, ready to empower them and raise them up. He will make them a part of His end-time Bride. Since this time, we have had salvations weekly. The people are coming to the Lord; He is drawing them with cords of love to Himself.

> *His lightnings lit up the world; The earth saw and trembled. The mountains melted like wax at the presence of the Lord, at the presence of the Lord of the whole earth. The Heavens declare His righteousness, and all the peoples have seen His glory. Let all those be ashamed who serve graven images, who boast themselves of idols; Worship Him, all you gods (Psalms 97:4-7).*

Chapter 22

Sounds of Heaven Growing Louder

April 8, 2013

I had a dream about Thea Jones, an old minister I knew in my youth. He was playing a harp. The harp rested on his chest and he supported the bottom with His left hand. He was strumming the harp like you would a guitar. Suddenly the harp shook in his hand with the presence of the Lord. I took the harp from him and began to play it. Only I played the harp by tapping the strings gently. The sound was so beautiful. I gave the harp back to the minister. He began to strum the harp again and all the strings broke with one swipe. It then caught on fire. I believe the face of worship will change and the old will be burned up.

April 11, 2013

Seymour had been doing a study on the names of God and how he shows himself to His church. I had been contemplating what he taught. One morning as I awoke, I asked the Lord how He was going to share Himself with us. I heard Him say, *"as Jehovah Tsidkenu"* (meaning, the Lord our Righteousness).

April 12, 2013

I was driving home from shopping and as I was driving I was praying about various things. Suddenly I saw a bomb in the air. I prayed, "Lord protect us, shield us and keep us safe!" Three days later a bomb went off in Boston, MA. There were 5 that did not go off, praise God.

This article's headline was posted on WND news site:

U.S. on Alert for Nuclear Blast Overhead 'Space Launch Vehicle' Could Kill Electric Grid, Devastate Nation

The article describes the threat of an EMP (Electromagnetic pulse) in addition to other recent news. Some excerpts:

> "...This concern is in addition to North Korea's latest threat to strike targets in Hawaii and the continental U.S., as well as possible attacks against U.S. bases in South Korea and Japan.
> "...The 28-year-old North Korean leader, Kim Jong-un, has signed an order for North Korea's strategic rocket forces to be on standby to fire at U.S. targets. The signing was against a photo backdrop following an emergency meeting of his senior military leaders showing large maps that were labeled "U.S. mainland strike plan, specifically at Hawaii, Washington, DC, Los Angeles and Austin, Texas." (One WND reader who traced the targeting to Texas said that it really was aimed at the Dallas/Fort Worth area) "...In recent weeks, North Korea also had released three videos showing a nuclear strike on the U.S."

April 18, 2013
I keep hearing this word: they (Afghans) want to make our country war-torn like theirs.

April 19, 2013

As we started the Prophet's Gathering, I saw the Angel of the Lord standing on my right. I was dressed in the same clothes as He was. Then I saw a huge whirlwind in the middle of room. The Lord said that everyone there would be able to hear Him. Then I saw a red sun; I watched this vision and wondered what it all meant. I continued to watch it intermittently as I worshiped. I felt in my heart I had thoughts that might be working against what the Lord wanted to say through me. I did not want to say anything negative, or speak of any coming judgment on the peoples. These words seemed to bring the soul down in fear.

I realized that I had to speak whatever He had to say or I was walking in disobedience to His will for me. I repented and again I saw the red sun. This time, white stripes appeared on the circumference. The stripes were wide at the end and narrowed toward the center. They covered the whole circle. I am not sure what it all meant, although I do know the red circle represented Japan. Then I remembered the Lord had said, *"Watch Japan."*

The Lord said to have the people come up and learn to listen for Him. The reason we were told to gather the prophets was to teach the people and train their spirits how to hear from Him. When Seymour came to speak the word, his face was lit up with the glory of the Lord. I saw that we were training people. At the end, the Lord spoke to anoint each person for this day and time.

April 21, 2013

I was being ordained and licensed along with two other ministers this Sunday. I had been ministering for 45 years and had never been officially ordained (I jokingly said I was not sent by the agency of man but by the Lord). Seymour heard from the Lord to pour the entire bottle of oil upon my head. The oil was called "the latter rain." The whole church was there and many came up and gave testimonies of what the Lord did through my life for them.

Suddenly I was in a vision. I saw myself in a dry, arid place with sandy colored mountains around me. I stood in the middle of the mountains. Somehow, the "real me" was observing from above watching myself below in this place. I could see everything from this vantage point. Demons began to clear out as soon as I stepped out on the ground. I knew it was a place the Lord was sending me. I saw black souls begin to come out and they followed me. These were captives of hell, and I was sent to break them out.

April 24, 2013

Seymour went to minister at my mother's church. Seymour had just finished his message and the pastor got up and began to exhort the people to worship the Lord. I raised my hands and began to tell the Lord how much I loved Him. He whispered, "I am with you." I was a little unsettled because of the vision I had earlier when I saw myself in the dry desert place. I knew it was the enemy's camp. I fell at the Lord's feet (my place of safety) and held on, not wanting to leave. He reached down and stood me on my feet before Him. I looked into His eyes and I saw a raging sea. For several days, I could see this sea in my mind's eye. I knew He was sending me to the sea of humanity. *Why do the nations rage when the King is on His throne?*

May 8, 2013

We were having home group, and during a moment of prayer I saw wings in the form of smoke fill the room. I watched as the wings came together and formed a flame that twisted together to form a large, fiery tongue. I wondered what this could mean.

May 17, 2013

We were at the Prophet's Gathering and I felt the Lord wanted us to pray in the Holy Spirit with speaking in tongues. As I continued to pray, Lord Holy Spirit began to teach me. He came and fell on the members of our body in a way that was uncontrollable:

> *So also the tongue is a small part of the body, and yet it boasts of great things. See how great a forest is set aflame by such a small fire! And the tongue is a fire, the very world of iniquity; the tongue is set among our members as that which defiles the entire body, and sets on fire the course of our life, and is set on fire by hell. For every species of beasts and birds, of reptiles and creatures of the sea, is tamed and has been tamed by the human race. But no one can tame the tongue; it is a restless evil and full of deadly poison (James 3:5-8).*

Scripture also says life and death are in the power of the tongue. The Lord showed me that what fell at Pentecost was tongues of fire for the purpose of redeeming the whole person of mankind.

> *And there appeared to them tongues as of fire distributing themselves, and they rested on each one of them. And they were all filled with the Holy Spirit and began to speak with other tongues, as the Spirit was giving them utterance (Acts 2:3-4).*

Lord Holy Spirit came to rule that little member that sets the flesh aflame with sin in order to bring life to our whole being. The Holy Spirit was deposited on the tongue to control and lead the whole person. So that what once was set on the fire of Hell is now set on the fire of Heaven; our whole person being trained for the purposes of God. If the Lord, through Lord Holy Spirit, controls our tongue, He controls our destiny. The tongue raises the Lord's righteous standard.

I began to see how important it is to let Lord Holy Spirit have control of our tongue—because we cannot control it on our own. Out of the abundance of our heart, the mouth speaks. The tongue has its own fire; it controls the entire body. Praying more in the spirit will discipline that little member and direct our whole being. It will change our hearts and make us more able to hear the Lord. When we are Spirit led, we are Heaven directed. Many times, people speak in the spirit one time and never practice it in prayer and as a way of prayer. WE MUST LET LORD HOLY SPIRIT HAVE CONTROL OF OUR TONGUE. IT IS THE VERY ESSENCE OF LIFE TO US IN HIM!

May 21, 2013
Jo-D and Cindi Hogan came and visited with us. At their first service, I was leading worship. Suddenly, I saw three doves flying in the atmosphere of the church. There was some warfare as I was leading. As I watched the doves flying, the church became electrified with the presence of the Lord. The sound became a sound from Heaven. The worship was glorious.

May 22, 2013
It was the second service with Jo-D and Cindi Hogan. Again I was leading worship. Again there was warfare in the atmosphere. Suddenly I saw a peaceful waterfall. As I continued to sing, bells came before me on my right. I began to strike them, and a beautiful sound rang out from them. I started singing about the bells. Colorful streamers began to fall; the presence of the Lord was in that place.

May 23, 2013
As I got into bed tonight, I saw an angel standing on my side of the bed. He had wings and a candle in his hand. His wings were very large and his left wing covered me. I wondered what this all meant. I saw this vision for several days.

May 24, 2013

As Seymour and I were before the Lord in prayer, I saw the angel again with the large wings. This time he wrapped me in His wings. Then the angel was gone and I was left with his wings. I laid in prayer wrapped in these wings. I looked like a piece of food you would put in the middle of lettuce leaves, with the lettuce folded gently around the food in the middle of it. I was resting peacefully. I soon began to see these wings begin to fold around me, covering me completely. These wings seemed to come in closer on me. I felt peace and wondered what the Father would impart to me next.

May 25, 2013

I awoke, and was sitting on the bed as I meditated on the Lord. I suddenly heard a trumpet blast in the distance. I have a trumpet sound as my ringtone on my cell phone (which was in the room), so I thought it was someone calling me. I went to answer it, but it was not my phone. I realized the sound of the trumpet was not in my bedroom. As soon as I walked out of the bedroom, I could hear the trumpet clearly. It was a shofar sound, with one long blast and then another blast. One hour after this, I was getting ready for church. I began to pray about having our people enter into fasting and praying, and as soon as this thought entered my mind I heard the shofar blast again, this time in my bedroom. I went into the next room where my phone was to see if it was my phone, but again, it was not. I went back into my bedroom and could hear the sound clearly again.

I remembered the day before when Seymour was teaching us out of the book of James, that suddenly the wind started blowing softly. We have chimes in our yard, and the wind blew the chimes. Those that were there heard the chimes. But Seymour heard something different. He asked, "Did anyone hear the trumpet blast?" We did not hear it, but he clearly heard it. I thought nothing about what he had heard, until this morning, when I was now hearing it. The Lord continued to take me deeper into this understanding of the sound of the trumpet.

May 27, 2013

A man in our church had a visitation from the Lord. The Lord spoke to him about the angels that were given seven trumpets.

May 28, 2013

We were in prayer, and I suddenly saw a very thick, silky, golden rectangular cloth floating down. The first one fell on me as I knelt before the Lord. Then I saw this cloth falling over and over again. Each time, I knew it was a new cloth falling. An angel came to stand by me, but I could not see his face, only his waist line. He had a rope-type belt with a key attached that was my focus. He took the key off and handed it to me.

May 29, 2013

As we prayed, I saw a hill where a winged angel was sitting on a horse. He had a silver trumpet to his mouth, and he was blowing it. I did not hear the sound of the trumpet, I only saw him.

May 30, 2013

Today, we went to minister and pray for a sister who had been near death. As we were talking to her she said, "Did you hear Gabriel blow the trumpet?" This woman is a new believer and has not read much of the Bible. I knew she would not know about such things. The Lord had me open to the book of The Revelation.

> *Then I saw the seven angels who stand before God, and to them were given seven trumpets. And another angel came and stood over the altar. He had a golden censer, and he was given very much incense (fragrant spices and gums which exhale perfume when burned), that he might mingle it with the prayers of all the people of God (the saints) upon the golden altar before the throne. And the smoke of the incense (the perfume) arose in the presence of God, with the prayers of the people of God (the saints), from the hand of the angel (Rev 8:2-4).*

The Lord is going to save many. We live in an adulterous generation, and sexual sin in the church is the norm. We must deal with it, as well as with the sins of bitterness and unforgiveness. Unforgiveness is the second sin (blaspheming the Lord Holy Spirit is the first) where Scripture states we will not be forgiven for our sins because of the Word not walked out in our lives.

And everyone who speaks a word against the Son of Man, it will be forgiven him; but he who blasphemes against the Holy Spirit, it will not be forgiven him (Luke 12:10).

But if you do not forgive others, then your Father will not forgive your transgressions (Matt 6:15).

Kingdom Keys

The Lord showed me that the trumpet blast was in relationship to prayer. It's the beginning of the pouring out of the bowls, which are the prayers of the saints. Many will have breakthroughs. This prayer will break the opposition to the saints. The Lord has shown me to pray more in the spirit. This would fill the bowls perfectly, because at times we do not know what to pray. The Spirit makes intercession for us beyond our words. PRAY SAINTS, PRAY!

The churches are filled with bitter, angry people praying unholy prayers against one another. These prayers never make it to the bowls of Heaven. Only pure and holy words spoken from the Father according to His will goes into these bowls. *This is the confidence which we have before Him, that if we ask anything according to His will, He hears us (1 John 5:14).*

The Father wants to raise up a holy standard of prayer warriors; cleansing all those who are in all types of filthiness and using them for His glory. We must fast and pray for the House of the Lord, that His righteousness will invade Earth and take away all guilt and stains from the Church. Lord Holy Spirit has the answers in prayer. He has the strategies to set all captives free.

June 1, 2013

Seymour and I were praying, and I saw a white horse whose rider was dressed in pure white. The whole scene glowed so brightly I could not see through it. The angel had a spear in his hand; the shaft of the spear was white but the tip of the spear was pure gold. He was pointing the spear toward us, as you would point out someone. We were kneeling before the Lord praying. I wondered if this was the appointed time for us.

June 12, 2013

As we held hands, the glory of the Lord filled the room. I saw a huge whirlwind in the middle of the room; I wanted to look inside it. I looked in, and the inside was golden and beautiful. I knew the Lord was telling us to stay in the center of the storm.

June 19, 2013

The Lord began to speak to me about our mouths; what we speak shows our hearts. The mouths of the people are so wicked. The more wicked the heart, the more wicked the speaking.

Later that day, I was editing my book. I read through some of the things the Lord had shown me. I began to realize how prophetic these words were. One vision in particular was a vision where I saw a golden lion. His head was at my feet and the tail was at my head. I had just read in Isaiah that the tail represented the prophets. I heard God speaking to me, calling me to be His prophet as in ancient days. I had no idea what this meant.

I began to pray, "Lord, if you want me to be your prophet, I accept your will." It was as if the Lord was waiting for me to accept this role. As soon as I said this, a man in a linen outfit appeared before me. He handed me a scroll that was covered in pure gold with writing on it. The scroll immediately went into two places—it went in my mouth and into the center of my being at the same time without dividing into two pieces. Then I saw Seymour, he was given a pure gold shepherd's staff. Gold suddenly appeared on his hands up to his wrists.

There appeared open mantles on our shoulders. These were thick mantles that had movement within them—like Jello when it wiggles, yet stretchy like a rubber band. It was an unusual material.

July 25, 2013

As we were praying at a friend's home outside Philadelphia, I saw the city's skyline. I then saw a lion in the air that roared. Then I saw a waterfall pouring over the city.

July 26, 2013

I was standing before the Throne of God, and I could see all the angels that were assigned to us. They were all around me as I stood before the throne. I saw the lion with eyes, I saw Raphael and the Revival Angel of Washington and others the Lord had sent. They were all touching me and strengthening me. I was crying out, "Lord! Please don't let me fail you, Lord!"

I then saw the Revival Angel of Philadelphia with a banner of red across his chest. He had a scroll in his left hand, which he handed to me. I took it and cradled it like a baby in my right arm. The scroll had an eagle on the top, and at the feet of the golden eagle there seemed to be a message that was part of the eagle. This was all gold, with a flap under the gold made of white paper. The throne had somehow moved, and I was looking at the earth. It was if angels like "fireflies" were flowing to the earth. I felt such power and authority from the Lord as I was being poured into.

August 2, 2013

As I was praying over the prayer meeting in the month of August, a golden whirlwind appeared in the room, kicking up dirt as it touched the ground. I could see the dirt fly up and around the bottom of the whirlwind.

August 22, 2013

We arrived in North Philadelphia where there was a gathering of pastors and leaders from various places in the United States who had heard that God was going to move in Philadelphia. They wanted to help a local church build a bigger building so that it would be able to house the people that would come.

The woman who was the pastor of the ministry was on the local TV and radio. Her church was small and could only fit about fifteen cramped people. But was situated on a much larger lot. It was decided that the new church would be built there.

During construction, a large tent was erected where the church began to hold services because the ministry was growing and needed more space. The pastor, a humble servant, had a vision for Philadelphia to be a part of the coming move of God. The Lord had given her favor with businessmen as well as leaders in the community and government officials.

As Seymour and I arrived at the tent the Lord spoke to me to walk the grounds. He then spoke to me to take off my shoes and walk the ground. I felt the presence of the Lord powerfully in one place in the tent; it was over in the left corner of the stage. I heard *"From the North, South, East, and West—call these forth!"* All weekend others heard the same. They blew the trumpets at the Liberty Straight Gate Church. The trumpets were blown to the north, south, east and west.

August 25, 2013

When I got up out of bed, the Lord said, *"The golden oil will flow from you and Seymour like golden oil trees."* I then saw into the heavenlies; I saw a tall figure with four wings. Later, I was in a tent meeting being held in Philadelphia. Seymour decided to go down to the front, so I went down and stood next to him.

Again, I saw the four winged creature, it was the ox. There were eyes all over him. I was seeing what he was seeing. He was looking in all directions at once. I could see people in pictures that looked like circles or bubbles. I could see their life and where they were. He was watching them. I knew they were being invited into being a sacrifice for the Lord.

I then saw a set of small, childlike hands reach out to me. I grabbed them, and I even hugged this ox. When I grabbed the hands, all of a sudden he went straight up and I went up with him. We were moving at a blazing speed, faster than the speed of light. Then we returned, and all the creatures surrounded me in a circle. All their hands were touching me. I saw the ox, then a man, then an eagle and finally the lion. I hugged the lion tightly and buried my face in his fur. I felt so much peace, so much joy—complete overwhelming joy.

Then all at once, we were all off again. There were four streams of light moving upward very fast. I believe all this moving faster than the speed of light was practice for me. I don't know exactly where we were going. I saw oil pouring down, peace pouring down, joy pouring down—Heaven was pouring down. It was awesome. I was so thankful that the Lord took me here. It was a holy place. I remember when I saw the two headed angel which looked in two directions (this was a vision I saw years earlier; the angel had two heads looking in opposite directions). The angel flew over the throne shouting, "HOLY, HOLY IS THE LORD GOD ALMIGHTY!" One head looked at the beginning of time, while the other head was looking to the end of the age, proclaiming that He was HOLY!! He is the Alpha and Omega, the beginning and the end.

The scene was surreal; I could feel the weight of glory everywhere. I looked around and nothing was the same. I could see what really was. I remember a week earlier, I heard Isaiah 42; I heard an audible voice that said, *"Open your eyes, open your eyes!"* I knew the Lord had opened my eyes. Everything seemed hollow and empty. I saw that the gifts we have are not in the fullness of what the Lord had planned. After a while, I felt a crown of fire on my head. My head was hot, burning with fire. *Lord, help us all to step into your fullness. We have not seen anything yet!* What is coming will be filled with more than we have seen; it will make the present Church seem hollow and empty. (I've since come to believe I was learning the scripture Jesus spoke of in The Lord's prayer, "as it is in heaven, let it be on earth.")

August 31, 2013
As I was going to sleep, I suddenly saw Raphael. He had a golden banner across his chest which is his usual outfit. He handed me a scroll covered in gold. Under the gold was pure white paper. I could see the heading on the page, it read "Seymour," the letters were written in gold. I took it from him. When I did, Seymour's name changed from gold to ink writing. Then gradually the name turned back to gold, all except part of the "r" at the end of his name. The Lord was turning everything about Seymour into gold; there was just a tiny bit to go before his life would be filled with the goldenness of God. I also saw Seymour and myself were dressed like Raphael. I could physically feel the golden banner as I lay in the bed.

September 2, 2013

I saw Seymour and myself step over into a new place with God. A completely new realm—it was like crossing over. I saw a wall between where we were and where we were stepping. It was like stepping into a new room.

September 7, 2013

I saw Seymour and me moving very quickly; at one time he was moving out front taking the lead, at other times I was moving out front. It was amazing; there were people following us, and they were moving fast as well. But we were out front leading.

September 10, 2013

I was watching as Obama was speaking and addressing the nation. He appeared to have horns on top of his head, and he took on a goat-like persona. He also had an earring in his ear. I am one who honors those in authority. The Lord says to pray for those who are in authority over you, and we must continue to pray for the man that the Lord put in the White House. Pray the will of God for him and not against him. In Jude 1, Michael did not bring a railing accusation against the enemy. But he spoke the will of God for that situation.

September 11, 2013

The Lord said, *"Listen to the book of My Revelation."* As I listened, John saw a book with seals, but no one could open the book. He began to cry, "Who can open the book?" The living creatures and the elders were there. There appeared a Lamb that was slain and the living creations and elders surrounded Him.

The Lord brought me back to the vision I had earlier of the living creatures surrounding me and touching me. The Lord revealed to me that they were not touching me per se, but they were touching the Lamb *in* me. Jesus. Who had been formed in me. I realized that Heaven is looking for Jesus formed in us. Heaven worked with the part of us that is like Jesus. Scriptures began to flood my mind, like, *Let this mind that was in Christ Jesus be also in you, Pick up your cross and follow me.* I knew as we become like Jesus we are walking out the Word. The Word in us becoming flesh, walking out Jesus, looking like Jesus, being like Jesus. How humbling and powerful this was to me.

September 13, 2013

I heard the word, "exponential." I knew it related to growth in God.

September 14, 2013

We were having our ladies meeting and one of the ladies was teaching. We take a theme, and stay on it for one year. This year's theme was "Moving with God as He Moves." We try to walk the Word out in our lives so that the Word becomes flesh and dwells in and around us. At this particular ladies' meeting the subject was how to walk in faith, and believe Him as He is moving with His attributes of faith. We were reading in James.

> *You believe that God is one. You do well; the demons also believe, and shudder. But are you willing to recognize, you foolish fellow, that faith without works is useless? Was not Abraham our father **justified by works** when he offered up Isaac his son on the altar? You see that **faith was working with his works,** and as a result of the works, faith was perfected; and the Scripture was fulfilled which says, "And Abraham believed God, and it was reckoned to him as righteousness"(James 2:19-23).*

The Lord spoke something to me that I had never seen before. I saw that Abraham was "justified by works" (not justified "by *his* works.") And the next sentence stated that "Faith was working with HIS WORKS. So that faith was a person and that faith came with something, and it was works—a perfect work. So that Faith works in us the will of God. It was completely different than I had ever read before.

The Lord said, *"Look at the next example that was given."* He was telling Abraham to offer his beloved son to Him. He said, *"How much tearing of his emotions do you think he went through? How much questioning of what I had said and promised, how much confusion in his own soul did he go through?"* We all would have gone through the same confusion and pain that he experienced. The Lord said that he was on a journey of faith his whole life. Faith led him to this place of a work that would be perfect before God. Beyond all his understanding, he gathered the wood. He laid his son on the altar. He reached for his knife and was going to plunge it into his son—and at the moment of complete surrender to the will of God, he was perfect. He was righteous; he overcame his fear, sorrow, and confusion concerning the promises of God. He laid it all down and he obeyed the Lord. At that moment Faith worked the work of perfection. So "Faith" has a work, and it perfects us in trusting God. Faith's work is to get our will to submit to His will before understanding why we are being tested in something. It requires absolute obedience to the Lord and His will. He wants us to put our will on the altar, letting it be crucified. What arises from this is righteousness and perfection in Christ, because we believe Him beyond ourselves and our promises, beyond our circumstances. We begin to say as Queen Esther said, "if I die, I die…". Either way, *I am going to see the King!* I am going to do His will no matter the cost to my emotions, my fears, even my death. I will obey and pursue Him."

This is the picture of seeking Him with all our heart. Just look at the Bible "Hall of Fame"—each person laid something down that would have an emotional, internal pull on the heart. From all practicality, they should have gone a different route to achieve the same goal, but they followed the way of God (to bring every thought into His Lordship, doing everything in His way). Doing His will, many times is a sacrifice of our soul's emotions. These are the works of faith when the height of our emotions can say, "Not my will, but your will be done." At that moment, we just purchased gold refined in the fire. Our hearts have become His heart. Our will is now His will, and we have been perfected, ready for every good work.

I realized that the Throne of the Lord was looking toward Earth. Heaven was searching the earth for those who would join the Hall of Fame and walk the faith of the ages. I want to join this Hall of Fame. Don't you?

Chapter 23

Living Beyond the Veil

October 12, 2013

The Lord spoke to me, *"Things have changed. You are moving into GRACE AND POWER."* The thing that was exciting to me is that we are moving into POWER. We are going to see the POWER OF GOD manifested in our lives. The Word of the Lord is going forth with power. No foe will stand before us because the very power of the Lord is going to stand up for us. This is the day of His power for us. Who can stand in the day of His power? *NO ONE CAN!* Because God is on the scene. God is taking control; those who believe will move with Him. True understanding of Grace and Power is that they are a team. When Grace shows up, Power shows up to back everything standing in the place that God will occupy. The Lord said you are FULL, FULL, FULL!

October 21, 2013

Seymour and I broke out into spontaneous prayer. I saw us having swords held high. We had on pure white gleaming armor, we were ready for war. I knew God was filling us with His grace and power to do His will.

October 27, 2013

I had a dream of a lot of people in a big room. Most were Christians, and they were doing what they wanted to do as far as working for the Lord.

They did what was comfortable and made them look good and feel excited. Another group of people came into this room. They were not saved and they made a lot of noise. The sound of their voices overpowered the sound of the Christians who seemed to be very quiet. All of a sudden, I fell on my face before the Lord and began to cry out in intercession. My voice became loud as I cried out to the Lord for souls. A sinner came near to my cry. He began to wonder about the cry and began to pay attention. I woke up.

I believe the Lord was saying that a lot of things that we do for the Lord make us feel good and make us look valid, but are not powerful enough to overtake or catch the eye of the sinner. In comparison, the sinners' sound is louder than the sound of the church. I saw that a cry of prayer is needed to come from the Church, a sound that would outweigh the cry of sin going up before the Lord. The intercession was uncomfortable and caused emotions that did not feel good, but these cries went up before the Lord. Nevertheless, these cries caused the sinners to pay attention, and they were attracted to the prayers. I also realized that the Lord was sending forth His sound in the earth. This sound was coming from Heaven. The earth is crying out against man and the sin of man. The Lord was looking for the cries of His people to go up and meet the cries coming down from Heaven. It is the place of "on Earth as it is in Heaven." The Lord is looking for those that will agree with Heaven.

Sin has a sound, and that sound is becoming louder than the cry of the intercessors standing in the gap and making up the hedge so that the Lord, in His righteousness, and His justice, has to come and strike the land. Prayer stand in the gap as Abraham did for Sodom and Gomorrah. The Lord came down to see if the sound that was coming before Him could be turned by His presence. Lot was in their midst enjoying the wealth, but not standing in the gap for the wicked people. He ended up with nothing but the shirt on his back and a next generation that could learn this lesson and do it right. God is looking for a sound that will come up before Him out of the Church. He will move for the sound alone. The sound of the true, a Church filled with faith, wanting His will not choosing their own lives. This means certain sounds are incomplete, certain sounds have mixture. God is looking to hear the pure sound of the Bride. THE PRAYERS OF THE BRIDE COMING UP BEFORE HIM.

THIS IS THE PLACE WHERE HEAVEN AND EARTH AGREE. If we pray according to His will He hears us.

That night, as I lay down to go to sleep, an angel stood beside my bed. He had a candle in his right hand and a sword in his left. I remembered the vision I had years ago when I saw an angel called Power. He looked the same (the candle and the sword). This time, he touched me with the sword. We need to walk in the light and power of God.

October 28, 2013

I was praying about spots on our garments and how to get rid of them. I saw a person standing with a white robe on, but there was dirt on the bottom of it. A fire started at the bottom of the robe and began to remove the dirt. I knew the Lord was saying the cleansing fire was the way the garment became white and clean. The things we go through are what cleanses and purifies our garments.

October 29, 2013

As I was getting into bed, I saw an angel with a candle and sword standing there. He placed his sword over me and Seymour as we slept. During midmorning as I awoke, I saw another angel with a sword in his hand. He was on Seymour's side of the bed. He placed his sword across Seymour and me from the other direction.

October 30, 2013

As I awoke in the morning, I heard the Lord whisper, *"You and Seymour are called to restore the Church."*

November 1, 2013

As I was leading worship, I heard the Lord say, *"I want to change my people's DNA."* We went back into worship and I saw two strands of DNA. The DNA strands were pure white and from the top down, the strands turned to pure gold. These strands were filled with the life and the power of God.

November 2, 2013

As I lay down to go to sleep, I saw a man dressed in a blue garment. I believe it was King David, although he was dressed as both a priest and a king. He came and laid his hand on my head. As I awoke, I saw myself feeding baby food to an adult. It was applesauce in a baby food jar.

Steps of Understanding
(Interpretation):

I received the interpretation as follows: The Lord is restoring the tabernacle of David. Whenever the Lord shows me a priest who is also a king, I know He is talking about a restoration of things to come. Restoring a people that worshipped the Lord as David did is the restoration of the Tabernacle of David! Those who have this anointed place must take the simplicity of true worship and break it down for musicians who have developed their gift of worship in a wrong manner. They have adopted the sounds and patterns of the world, offering this up as worship to the Lord.

The enemy of this world has a tight stronghold on the sound that goes forth. It is used to control the masses and manipulate the hearts and minds of the listeners. This sound is all about self and flesh. It is self-focused, feeding the emotions and the will of people. It counterfeits the worship experience, preventing people from being able to enter into true intimacy with the Lord. Unless one chooses against self, true intimacy seems strange, unfamiliar and uncomfortable to the hearer.

Worship should not be about us, but about bringing a person into "oneness with the God of Heaven." Worship is ministering to the Lord. The Lord once spoke to me that I could not minister to people until I learned first to minister to Him. The Church has gotten comfortable with its style of worship, have grown up in this type of atmosphere. They can only receive a little bit of the true Tabernacle of David type worship, because they are not able to digest it. They are like a child whose digestive system is not developed enough to eat solid food. This is a powerful warfare type of worship, meant to be taught to the musicians. It is beyond human understanding. It has a perfect sound that they were made for. Unfortunately, the enemy snaps them up in their youth. Unless they are willing to forsake all and follow the Lord in their sound, *they will never hear it.* They *must* be discipled by Heaven. We don't understand that this world has discipled every thought, every sound, every move we have made before our salvation and we must be made anew. If we are still acting like the old man, we have yet to put on the new.

> *For if anyone is a hearer of the word and not a doer, he is like a man who looks at his natural face in a mirror; for once he has looked at himself and gone away, he has immediately forgotten what kind of person he was. But one who looks intently at the perfect law, the law of liberty, and abides by it, not having become a forgetful hearer but an effectual doer, this man will be blessed in what he does (James 1:23-25).*

November 3, 2013

I was leading worship. I saw myself before the Throne, when suddenly a golden smoke wrapped around me--a combination of incense and liquid gold. As I worshiped the Lord, He was covering me in liquid gold. It was beautiful and had a lovely fluidity. I felt love so deep, and the kingship of the Lord was reigning over me. I began calling out for the Lord to dig a deep well within me. I saw a new river springing up and flowing out of my innermost being.

November 13, 2013

We were at home group, and as we were ending in prayer I saw an open Heaven over us. I heard, *"Come up here."* I saw myself by the Throne of God looking out over the world. I had two thunderbolts coming out of my mouth that were to be spoken out over the earth. I heard the Lord say to me, *"I have called you and appointed you and I am watching over your heart."*

November 15, 2013

We were sitting out in our car, looking at our house. I heard the Lord say, *"The plans for your house will be approved on Monday."* Monday came and we got a call at 3:30 that the plans for the house had been approved.

Wolves in the House
November 20, 2013

The Lord spoke to me about wolves among the flock. I then had a dream about people who were gathered together in one place. In this place, there were many doors that you could choose from. I was standing in a hallway looking at the closed doors. Suddenly, a man came out of one of the doors. As I looked at him, he turned into a huge wolf. He stuck out his tongue, and I saw that it was forked, like a snake's. I also saw that the tongue had a lot of garbage and dirt on it. He licked me with his tongue, and I suddenly felt so good all over. It was not a heart-felt goodness, rather it was flesh satisfaction. It was like getting in a Jacuzzi or getting a facial or massage at a spa. It was petting and stroking the flesh. He then went back through the door he came out of and turned back into a man. He sat down and had a little boy in his lap. He looked like a good father, one to be admired and respected. I looked around the room and there were many such people. I heard, *"There are wolves among the church."* Then I awoke.

I knew the Lord was saying the Church is filled with wolves. The Lord opened one door and let me see the real nature of the wolf. This wolf is speaking a lot of lies that are not Truth. The lies are making people feel good in their soul. They are not telling people the Truth that sets them free from the bondage of a lie or training them to stand in coming days that are just ahead of us. Their truths are relaxing the church, massaging their egos and speaking words that lull them to sleep so that they are not on guard. They are raising up children who are doing the same. They are leaders and people that look good according to our natural point of view. They are saying all the right things and doing what society deems proper and correct. They are not going against the status quo or raising up people of the Kingdom of God. We are not of this world or its systems. We are a royal priesthood with its own way of moving in God that is different from this world system. Each of us is called to move with God according to our piece of the puzzle, which—when complete—will look like Jesus.

Then the Lord said, *"The wolves have crept in unaware."* This alarmed me, because I thought, *how did we not know?* I said, "Lord, I want to know." He spoke to me, *"This is how you will know whether a person has the potential to be a wolf or not."* He took me to the two priests in Ezekiel 44. One priest was not loyal to the

Lord. Because he was not faithful, the Lord said, "You will not come before me to minister to me, but you will minister before the people."

Then the Lord instructed the sons of Zadok how they were to come and minister to Him. They were not to sweat before Him; they had a "no sweat" ministry. They were to come near to Him to worship and listen to Him. As they did this, they became holy before Lord and were pleasing in His sight. The Lord is looking for the no sweat ministry. He wants us to minister to Him and to love being with Him. He does not want us to love the praises of men and their thoughts on what should be done, but to honor the Father above all. His ear is listening for the Spirit of God, not the cries of men and women who want their way. The Father was teaching me that anyone who wants their ministry but does not want to be intimate with Him first, has the potential to become a wolf. Because they will, at some point, choose their life rather than His ways. Even those who start out with pure motives and intentions can be derailed if they have not dealt with the ways of self. The Lord said, "The Holy Spirit is not in competition with Himself." If we are of the Spirit, we will have unity with one another. The Spirit of God draws together those that are His.

Next, He took me to John the Baptist. John was not like the priests of his day. He did not buy into the systems that the priests had laid down for gaining the hearts and minds of the people. John's location, dress, and even what he ate was different than the priests of his day. The Lord was saying through John's life: *I am coming in a different way than you expect. Can you see it? You must decrease in all that you are, so that the new thing I am doing can take hold of you.* John knew that he was a forerunner of the Messiah, the spirit of Elijah was on him. The true spirit of Elijah that is in the earth again understands decreasing in every way so that the Messiah can be brought forth in power. The Lord was showing me that anyone not willing to decrease their soul, their ministry, their reputation—if and when the Lord requires --has the potential of being a wolf. I must decrease in order for Him to increase in me. This was the heart of John the Baptist, a preparer of the way of the Lord.

He understood it was not about Him; it was about the one he was preparing the people for. Scripture says that the Pharisees did not receive the baptism of John therefore they were not prepared to receive Jesus when He came.

John preached, "Repent and be baptized, every one of you." Those who heard John received and believed. Those that did not hear, did not have the grace to receive Jesus because what was being given was the preparation for "the Day of the Lord." Again, the spirit of Elijah is preparing a people to receive the coming of the Lord!

Saints, I believe the next two years are going to be a game changer for all of us, especially Israel. The day of great evil is on the land like never before. This is the time when God's people must know Him intimately in order to stand. For if we stand, we will walk in His power. Everything we believe will be called into the fire. If we are overwhelmed by little trials while we are at peace, what will we do when everything seems to be against us? What will we believe then? To the degree that the Word (Jesus) has been formed in us is the degree we will stand. We must walk out the chapter of love in Corinthians in our flesh and in our everyday life. We must drink in the many scriptures that need to be put into our flesh and walked out. Start with one, and ask the Holy Spirit to lead you till you live it from the secret place where Deep calls to deep.

November 21, 2013

We were at the gate in Charleston with a brother we had just met days earlier. We prayed in a circle with others who were also there. I saw a shaft of light come down; I had seen this light many times before. This time an angel appeared in the shaft of light. He had a sword in his left hand with a hilt of white which he held up toward the heavens. The sword was pure gold, and it gave off a light so brilliant it was blinding, so that the eye could not focus and the angel was barely visible. The sword was the centerpiece of the vision. We prayed again, and this time I saw a wall of water coming off of the battery; it was coming as a force, slicing the buildings in half and destroying them. *(Note: I believe the Lord was showing me a picture related to a flood that came at the end of 2015 or 2016).*

December 6, 2013

We were having prayer, and I heard the Lord say *"Pray for all to be released from mind control."* I saw that as a nation we were all under mind controlling forces. Commercials get people to buy things that don't really work, and they don' really need. Society spends much time and many dollars studying humanity to see what they can get us to respond to. The Lord wants us to be free from all forms of worldly controlling spirits. I saw this was a form of witchcraft, directing humanity like zombies.

As we prayed, I reached my hand up and I saw the fiery hand of the Lord reach down and grab my hand. Then I saw a dark fog over the earth; it was filled with darkness and evil. The Lord lifted us up above it all and we could see clearly. Above the fog, the sky was blue and the air was fresh. I prayed that we could help lead others out of where they are; to go above the stench of this earth.

December 8, 2013

I have seen this vision many times. In it, Then I see the eyes of the Lord looking throughout the earth for those who look like Him in their hearts. They are the ones who dare to stand out against the evil that is around them, saints who refuse to walk by the dictates of society. He is looking for those who are seeking the original design that He put in them. Noah was righteous in his generation; He lived among an evil and depraved people. Noah was found righteous because he had learned the ways of God, and honored Him. We were fervent in prayer this Sunday. Seymour was ministering on John the Baptist's birth and who he would be: the spirit and power of Elijah. As he was speaking, I heard the Lord say, *"Take off your shoes."* Suddenly, Seymour took off His shoes and then I saw Jesus walking back and forth in front of Seymour. He was watching us as he taught. Lord, let me hear what is being said and walk it out.

December 11, 2013

As Seymour and I were before the Lord praying, I saw a shaft of golden light come down on our innermost being. Then I saw us covered in gold.

December 14, 2013

Seymour and I went for a walk. As we walked, we were praying, and suddenly we saw a burst of light. It was midnight, so it was pretty dark outside. The distance from us was as a bird flying over the trees. We saw it out of our peripheral vision, and both of us thought it must have been a meteor. It was truly amazing to see something glowing so close to us.

December 15, 2013

I heard these words and I began to type what I heard. I believe the Lord is speaking of a great change coming over the whole world, especially Israel. Life as we know it will change for many. We are going see more and more judgments being poured out on Israel and the Church. Some in the Body will come alive in power, while others will perish and fall away because of their lack of faith and the false doctrine they have embraced.

They did not have the ways of God, so they began to resent the Lord and His ways. They will be angry because they thought the Lord should have delivered them and deliverance did not come, so they will begin to lose heart, and ultimately their faith. It is the time of the great falling away. While the old Church is falling away, many will be running to the Kingdom to learn the ways of God in the midst of adversity. These new converts will learn quickly how to walk with the Lord in His power. They will see His signs and wonders.

Israel will see much war and devastation. A day of great repentance will come upon her, and she will again remember the God of her fathers. Many in Israel will turn to the Lord and repent for the evil done in the land. They will be greatly persecuted by those of a hardened heart, but the Lord will act on their behalf.

This is a time when the Lord will move in great power. Many will see the salvation of the Lord supernaturally. Television will broadcast some of these wonders, and the eyes of many will be open to the Lord. Seeds planted by praying parents and grandparents will burst forth in these days. The Lord will also save some so-called atheists. As hard as they were *against* Jesus, they will become firebrands *for* Him, even as Paul did once he saw the Truth. People in witchcraft and demonic filth will be delivered and exchange their illegal seeking of power for the true power which is Jesus. They shall be beautifully set free and delivered. 2014 will be a year of more extremes, and we will begin to see dramatic changes in people and countries.

Backsliding sinners will rush into the house of the Lord, and He will use many of them to start churches fresh and anew, because many places of worship will close down. The government will crack down on churches with 501c3 status, and force them to comply with state and federal mandates. These churches let the government in, and at some point they will take possession and find reasons to close them down or shape them ultimately into state run churches. They will start to do this by making demands on churches to adopt secular programs and unbiblical practices. Some will go along with it to keep their doors open, but because they did not stand for the Lord, He will write ICHABOD on the doors and the place will close by the finger of God. Others will refuse, and they will close. From the ashes of a Church that has been burned up, a new, more powerful church will arise in glory and strength. The Spirit of Elijah will be upon the land, and the remnant Church will be ready to hear the Word of the Lord, and to follow it.

We will see the winds of change blowing in government and in culture, things happening on an unprecedented level and extreme ideas being forced upon us *(Later note: I believe ISIS came on the scene at that time—whoever thought we would see people beheaded and burned alive on TV or YouTube? It is happening in places where the Church is coming under persecution).*

Wealth will be removed from many families. Out of this will come salvation and dependence upon the Lord. Many will be humbled by the hand of the Lord. It will be a time of the refining all things, preparing a people to come before Him. He will try the hearts of people and countries to see what is in them. Hold onto the Lord and trust Him always. We will need to trust Him just like those who trusted the Lord in great adversity; those taken to concentration camps who believed God after they were put into the hands of satan through the Nazis. They trusted the Lord unto death. Be strong and hold on to the Lord.

After writing down what I heard, I saw a bright light but did not see anyone in the light. I heard these words: "My name is Gabriel and I am here to help." I then saw a second bright light, and I heard: "On the third day, you will lose the weight." I thought, *Am I going to have supernatural weight loss?* I pondered these words all day, wondering what they meant. At 3:35 PM, Seymour was ministering at church. I knew the time specifically because I was looking at my iPad as he taught, following the scriptures with him. Suddenly, I became very cold. I thought I was catching a flu or bug that had been going around. I had the church pray for me to be healed. I went home and got under two heating blankets, a sleeping bag and a fur throw, but the coldness would not leave. Around 11:45 PM, I was feeling like I could not breathe, so I got up to use a decongestant. As I got up, I suddenly felt my mother. I was walking like my mother. It was as if I *was* my mother. I told Seymour what I felt, because it was such a strange feeling. Again, I pondered...*what did it mean?*

At 12:30 AM, I got a call that my mother had died. She had gone home to be with the Lord at 11:45 PM. I was reeling in shock and disbelief at the news. The next day, I began to make all the arrangements for my mother's funeral. My family and my mother's church needed to view the body. Her church had been there for her many times when Seymour and I were not able to go to Atlanta and be by her side.

The next day, we had a memorial for her following cremation. The following day, we drove her to Mobile, Alabama, where we were to scatter her ashes. On the third day of our 3-day journey, I "lost the weight,"—the weight of responsibility lifted just as I had heard in my vision. I had not realized how heavy the burden was I had been carrying. The Lord knew how close I was to my mother, and He graciously sent me help from on high, because I was truly devastated by her death.

Through this experience I learned about the importance of honor. The Lord said, *Honor your mother and father, that your day will be long upon the land.* How we honor our parents is how we will honor God. The whole process of laying my mother to rest was one of honoring her. It was not about my grief, it was about doing things God's way, stepping into His principles for the God life. If I have honor toward my parents, I would honor God, and out of that honor I would walk in righteousness. That righteousness would create greater longevity in my body (your days will be long upon the land).

This honor needs to come from the heart—it is not mechanical or co-dependent. It is honoring their life, and who they were to us. When my mother died, all memories or thoughts that were not the best of our time together went away, because all was forgiven. The only thing that was left was the good that her life represented.

Chapter 24

Preparing for the Final Revival and Harvest

January 10, 2014 [7]

It was 1:30 AM and Seymour and I were about to fall sleep. I saw a big angel standing over us. He held a sword in both hands, close to his body and pointed upward. The hilt of the sword was pure gold, and the blade was pure silver. He then stretched the sword out over us horizontally. I noticed the sword was about six feet long, because it stretched down below our feet. He pulled the sword up again. This happened several times.

We were at a meeting, and communion was being prepared by the leaders. I closed my eyes in prayer. Suddenly, I saw living light coming toward me. The light moved with the presence of God. Then I saw a golden box that glowed with the light of the Lord. I saw hands holding the box. The presence of the Lord was so brilliant I could hardly see who was holding the box. I knew he was a priest of the Lord, because I had seen him before. (It was as though he was a priestly king; I had the sense it was King David).

---

[7] *A week before I was to meet with my editor, all the 2014 visions stored on my iPad were lost. I had been using the Cloud service to store my book, but they somehow disappeared right before my meeting. Seymour had heard from the Lord to write down things the Lord was showing me. I wondered why he was doing this, because he had never done it before. Thank God he did, because we were able to piece together much of what the Lord sent but satan had tried to steal. The warfare over the 2014 visions (and the entire book) has been testing our faith and ability to stand for God wants no matter the cost. I am actually honored to be considered such a threat by the enemy that he would devote such effort to derail this work.*

The priest had an outer blue robe with a pure white robe underneath. The box he held was about 17 inches wide and 8 inches tall, with a beautiful design covering it. The box was being handed to me, so I took it in the natural realm, and I knew it was to replace the bowl that was given to me so many years ago by the Revival Angel of Charleston. I believe the Lord was showing me dimensions of worship being gifted, like the bowl of intercession on Anson St.. This was a new release that would be filled with gifts and glory.

January 12, 2014

During Sunday's worship time, I again saw this bright, living light. The box was no longer there, because I now had it within me. This time, a hand reached out from the light, and I saw a ring that I knew was a signet ring on the hand of Jesus. It was His left hand, and as He reached toward me, I saw that the stone was oblong, and looked like a Jasper stone. The color was amber and it was beautiful, but it was not in an ornate design. It looked rather plain. I grasped His hand, and he gave it to me. Later that evening at home group, I saw a vision that I was standing on a flat whirlwind. I was holding hands with Seymour, and he was standing below the whirlwind. Suddenly he moved up above me while we were still holding hands. Then he came down and was level with me on top of the whirlwind. Then we both moved upward together.

February 4, 2014

We began a prayer time called The 60-day Challenge, put out by Dennis and Jen Clark. The Lord had sent this to us as a next step in Him. As we began, the Lord spoke to me and said, *You must release all the burdens you have been carrying for years*. I knew I was a burden bearer. God puts burden bearers in His house to discern and pick up in the spirit those who are carrying weights too heavy for them to bear. The burden bearer will suddenly think on someone out of the blue, and their job is to lift up to the Lord those people that need immediate help from on high. The problem comes when burden bearers are very close to people, like family or friends. Instead of staying steady emotionally, the burden bearer can go into worry and fear, which often results in them not being able to let go of the burden. They are to carry the burden to Jesus, release it and leave it there. They need to always remember they are a helper, not a savior. There is only one

Savior, and that is Jesus. The Lord wants the burden bearer to carry all things to Him in prayer, thereby assisting those who are in need of a boost up from where they are. The Lord has such a beautiful system for the body of Christ to operate by. So the Lord spoke to me to release all these burdens. I knew I was carrying so many things that they had become a vague but massive and draining load. So much so, that I did not want to discern one more thing from another person. I would avoid people unless the Lord ordered me because I felt I could not take in one more thing. From this place, the Lord spoke: *Cast it all on me.* I did, and suddenly I felt such freedom! I was emptied, and able to be filled afresh. He was preparing a new container within me to hold something more complete in Him.

February 9, 2014

As I was leading worship this day, I was expressing to the Lord how much I loved Him. He said, *Now, I want you to feel MY love.* I had felt His love many times before. This time it was different. His love was complete and holy. His love was filled with purpose. The next day Seymour and I lay praying before the Lord. Again, the Lord spoke: *Feel my love.* I felt His love again. This time, I saw that the whole universe was held together by His love. Everything that was created was created out of His love. I understood that His love was more than a feeling—His love was *everything* and *everywhere.*

I saw that His love could bless and curse all at the same time—that when judgment came on the earth, it was His love that brought it. I only use that example because we all relate love to that which is good for us. If someone loves us then they will do only good toward us. But the Lord's love did what was good for us. *I saw that with our love we can work for the Lord, but with God's love we can do the works of God.* I suddenly understood that I needed to move in His love. Not as I understood it, but as His will wanted it to unfold before His people. There was a situation of offense I was praying about that my love was not enough to overcome. The Lord said, *Let my love flow to it and through it.* I did as the Lord instructed, and His love flowed so completely out of me that I could not remember to feel the offense. I saw the power in His love when it flowed, and that everything and anything could be accomplished when it flowed.

February 11, 2014

I saw angels that were surrounding me like a cord of wood. It was like a wall in an old American fort, a wall of protection. They had swords that were trumpet and their trumpets were swords. I then saw a man hovering in the air, dressed in white. I did not have a good feeling about him, his clothes made him look like a flying squirrel. I sensed in the vision the person had a religious spirit, but knew the angels were a guard around me. Within minutes after prayer, a person showed up at the door to complain about something we did. We told the truth of the matter and the person felt silly that the issue was even brought to us. He gave us a word from the Lord that the Lord had given me earlier, which was that the Lord was polishing us. It was beautiful how the Lord turned it all around.

February 12, 2014 I saw into Heaven, and then I went up to a new place in Heaven. I saw a set of pearl steps that led to a room that was filled with weapons. In the room I saw a sword that glowed with the power of God. Seymour was standing in the doorway looking out. I reached for the sword and it was in my hand suddenly.

March 11, 2014

In prayer, I saw a vision over, and over, and over again. In it, I am outside the earth seeing the universe. I am all white, and the man of the four living creatures has his left hand on my right shoulder (judgment given, grace to understand and bear the government of Jesus to His peoples.) He is the one who is showing me all this. Suddenly, I see a meteor with a tail, but I do not know if it is going to hit the earth. I see a comet, on fire, headed to the earth, then I see bombs going off—little lights. I ask where—I'm told Turkey. I somehow sense that the earth is dying, then see that the earth and the universe are coming into an alignment. Over my head, seven silver trumpets appear and are pointed toward the earth. I then see a man with eyes all over him, opening up my eyes for me to see (his hand upon my shoulder for this). What does this man with all the eyes represent? God answered, *To see man in his ways. To SEE the ways of MAN.*

This vision repeated itself over and over again. First the meteor—I don't know if it is going to hit. Then the bombs over Turkey, then the earth dying, the alignment of the earth and universe with the seven silver trumpets. The Lord is coming—I saw the Lord riding on a horse, somewhat far away. Waves of things coming toward the earth. The whole time, scriptures kept coming. They were given to warn about what is ahead and to help us prepare the saints of God to walk in this end-time. I believe the vision kept repeating because these signs would happen over and over again. Following are the scriptures that I head and their meaning.

> *Knowing that whatever good thing each one does, this he will receive back from the Lord, whether slave or free Ephesians 6:8*

The Lord was speaking of a great revival coming. He was going to move on the save and the unsaved He was going to cause many to come to into the Kingdom. This was going to be a move of God.

> *I say to you, it will be more tolerable in that day for Sodom than for that city. Luke 10:12*

He was saying to these people that there will be those that will not receive the move of God. He will judge them.

> *For if Joshua had given them rest, He would not have spoken of another day after that. Hebrews 4:8*

He was saying to the people that He moves upon. Tho you see these things don't be afraid rest in the Lord. Be at peace. This is the day of learning to rest in Him that He is doing all that we see and hear. Don't fear be at rest in your souls. Psalms 91, but especially Psalms 91:8. You will see with your eyes…

> *The sky was split apart like a scroll when it is rolled up, and every mountain and island were moved out of their places. Revelation 6:14*

We are going to see signs in the heavens and on the earth again don't fear. The Lord is saying this is my doings. Rest and pray, your life is in His hands.

> *Trust in the Lord with all your heart and do not lean on your own understanding. 6 In all your ways acknowledge Him, and He will make your paths straight. Proverbs 3:5-6*

This is the times of resting in the Lord so that your steps may be ordered. We will not know how to step or where is the safe place to abide in. Let Him direct you. Pray and move as He says move. Learn to move with Him!

> *So I was left alone and saw this great vision; yet no strength was left in me, for my natural color turned to a deathly pallor, and I retained no strength. But I heard the sound of his words; and as soon as I heard the sound of his words, I fell into a deep sleep on my face, with my face to the ground.*
>
> *Then behold, a hand touched me and set me trembling on my hands and knees. He said to me, "O Daniel, man of high esteem, understand the words that I am about to tell you and stand." Daniel 10:8-14*

The Lord was saying that there are things that I would see that would make me fearful, and I have seen many things that have caused my heart to tremble. The Lord was speaking to me personally that I was given grace to see and to walk with Him where He wants to go.

July 8, 2014

The Lord said, indeed the fire of His presence is present, and it is coming to wash away the guilt from His house. The fire will increase to such intensity that the people of the Lord will cry out with a repented heart. Sinners will be coming into the house of the Lord. The Lord is coming in unapproachable light, which will thoroughly cleanse His House (*Psalms 89:14)*. The first wave of fire is a cleansing wave. The second wave of fire is a power wave to equip the saints. The third wave of fire will gather those who WILL gather. The next wave after this is Joel's outpouring for those who have yielded to the fire. To get through the first wave of fire, we must be thankful, yielding, and repenting. Open your heart up to the will and purposes that will be coming from the Lord in order to prepare the heart. This first cleansing will prepare the heart to hear and obey. It will also cause a rest in the soul, which will cause assurances to come to people's heart, so that they will know that the Lord is with them.

*I acknowledged my sin to You, and my iniquity I did not hide. I said, **I will confess my transgressions to the Lord [continually unfolding the past till all is told]—then You [instantly] forgave me the guilt and iniquity of my sin. Selah [pause, and calmly think of that]!** For this [forgiveness] let everyone who is godly pray—pray to You in a time when You may be found; surely when the great waters [of trial] overflow, they shall not reach [the spirit in] him. You are a hiding place for me; You, Lord, preserve me from trouble, You surround me with songs and shouts of deliverance. Selah [pause, and calmly think of that] Psalms 32:5-7)!*

The second wave will cause the ability not to move ahead of God but wait on His Power. His Power will take cities and regions.

*The last wave of fire will cause them to see the Kingdom Mandate begin to come forth and a working together in unity, honoring one another's gifts. Because the King has a team that can be used mightily, waiting for the show of unusual signs and wonders, they will not take the glory and touch it and will demonstrate how to move with God.

So to recap:

- First fire will correct

- Second fire will empower

- Third fire will gather for the preparation of the greatest move, the former and the latter rain: the mighty River of God

Blessings to all who read this. May you prepare your hearts for His coming!!!

The Purifier

Behold, I am going to send My messenger, and he will clear the way before Me. And the Lord, whom you seek, will suddenly come to His temple; and the messenger of the covenant, in whom you delight, behold, He is coming," says the Lord of hosts. But who can endure the day of His coming? And who can stand when He appears? For He is like a refiner's fire and like fullers' soap. He will sit as a smelter and purifier of silver, and He will purify the sons of Levi and refine them like gold and silver, so that they may present to the Lord offerings in righteousness. Then the offering of Judah and Jerusalem will be pleasing to the Lord as in the days of old and as in former years (Mal 3:1-4)

March 2, 2016

I was awakened at 3 AM. This wakefulness was significantly different than any I had ever experienced up to this time. People who have had a near death experience testify that they have felt a heightened sense of awareness, which would believe is very similar to what I felt. It happened after we had attended meeting the Sunday night prior at a local church that was gathering for the purposes of unity.

I wondered whether or not the changing of the guard took place, and we were like the watchmen. The Lord had already spoken to us that the "changing of the guard" was coming. I heard the word Watchmen as I was awakened. I knew my spirit was awakened on a heightened sensory level.

Interestingly, I had not added a period to my sentence when I had the thought to put it through the grammar checker. I reread what I had typed then copied and pasted it into the grammar checker. What the checker reflected astonished me! noticed a line had been added. I had not typed this line but yet the line was there.

To all who read this: may you prepare your hearts of His coming!!!

Steps of Understanding

(Interpretation):
The reason I believe the Lord used the words "OF" instead of "FOR". Is because He was not talking about the Rapture. He was speaking about THE DAY OF THE LORD! The word about the 3 levels of fires that are coming and the dream of being awaken to a new level were the same message. I realized the Lord was speaking to us to prepare for His showing up.
God is saying to us,
"Prepare your hearts."
This is a spiritual awakening. God is awakening us!!!

Many visions and revelations are continuing to come forth—too many to be put in this book. So the story continues…

My Prayer for You...

Would be for you, my friends, to also experience an increase in encounters with your Lord, including His dreams and visions for you. May you know the Lord's intimate love for you, and walk with Him heart to heart. May you be deeply aware of His presence in every aspect of your life, and may your whole being embrace the depths of revelation that He has for you. I want to pray an impartation of Lord Holy Spirit to open your eyes of understanding, and your heart to receive all that He desires to reveal to you. I pray that purity would be the banner over your life, because Jesus said, *"The pure in heart shall see God."* I pray that reading the journal reports from my journeys between Heaven and Earth will stir up the gifts within you, and prepare you for the adventure of your life!

All honor be to Jesus ,the King of Glory!
AMEN!

59942621R00137

Made in the USA
Charleston, SC
19 August 2016